Jeremiah
God's Messenger to an Antagonistic People

Bob McDoniel

James Kay Publishing

Tulsa, Oklahoma

This book is an uninspired work
and is intended to be used as a study guide
alongside the inspired work of prophecy.
The thoughts, suggestions, and comments
are the result of the author's study.

Jeremiah
God's Messenger to an Antagonistic People
ISBN 978-1-943245-04-8

www.jameskaypublishing.com

e-mail: sales@jameskaypublishing.com

© 2015 Bob McDoniel
Cover design by JKP
Author Photo by Dorothy McDoniel

All rights reserved.
No part of this book may be reproduced in any form or by any means
without permission in writing from the author.
The cover contains an image of a portion of a Dead Sea Scroll, this
does not contain the text of Jeremiah, but is simply used as an illustration.
All diligence to find the source of this image
concludes it to be in the Public Domain.

Dedication

This work is dedicated to the memory
of two faithful messengers of God:

Glen McDoniel

and

Batsell Barrett Baxter

Preface:

This book began as a set of teaching notes for an adult Sunday morning Bible class. At the outset I had as my goal to glean the message of the book for myself then present my understanding to the class. To accomplish this goal I did not consult any commentary but instead read the text from three or four English translations of the Bible and then made my notes from my understanding of the text. Near the end of the class several students asked for copies of my notes so they could have them for future study. At that time I simply made photo-copies of my typed notes. Since that time I have tried to clean up some of the typographical errors that existed in that original copy with the thought in mind that these notes might be helpful to others. Please understand that I do not consider myself to be an expert on Old Testament prophecy nor am I a language scholar. My intent in publishing these notes is to spur further study. If this work encourages you to study for yourself and can be a help in understanding the willingness of Jeremiah to deliver God's message to the people of his day even when it meant standing alone, then I will have more than achieved my goal. Jeremiah is a book with applications for faithful servants of God even today. May we be encouraged by this young prophet's humility and dedication.

Robert McDoniel

Introduction

Jeremiah lived approximately 100 years after Isaiah. Where Isaiah had been able to save Jerusalem from Assyria, Jeremiah was unable to turn Judah and save them from Babylon. This book is one of the final efforts to turn Judah back to God before they were taken into Babylonian captivity. Jeremiah's job was a difficult one. For over 40 years he delivered a message of doom to a stiff-necked people. Jeremiah dates many of his messages but the book is put together more topically than chronologically. The message is clear. "Surrender to God is the only way to escape the upcoming calamity."

This book was dictated to and written down by a man named Baruch. The writing of these prophecies dates to the fourth year of Jehoiakim.

Chapter 1

vv.1-3 In these verses Jeremiah introduces himself and dates the time of his ministry. Jeremiah is young and from a family of priests. Anathoth is about 2 miles north of Jerusalem. Hilkiah was the priest who found the book of the law while repairing the temple and took it to Josiah as recorded in **2 Kings 22**. This gives Jeremiah a strong background. He will begin delivering God's message to Judah during the reign of Josiah and continue until after they are taken into captivity.

v.4 This book is God's message to this wayward people.

v.5 It was God's plan that Jeremiah be a prophet even before his birth. This points up the personhood of an individual even before birth. God knows the future as well as the present and the past. God has a plan for every life. It is up to us to decide to live our lives according to God's plan.

v.6 Jeremiah was still very young (some believe under 20) when God called him to carry out this mission. Contrast Jeremiah's argument to Moses' excuses when God called him which are recorded in Exodus chapters three and four.

vv.7,8 These verses record God's answer to Jeremiah's youth excuse. It did not matter that Jeremiah was young. He was sent by God, he was delivering God's message, and God was going to be with him. (See Paul's declaration in **Phil 4:13**)

v.9 God then touches Jeremiah's lips. How is this different from Isaiah's lips being touched with the live coal in **Isa. 6**? Isaiah's touch was a cleansing touch and Jeremiah's was a commissioning touch. He was being given the words he was to say.

v.10 At this point Jeremiah is being challenged by God to go to the nations. Jeremiah's prophesies against the nations will be seen in chapters 46-52.

vv.11,12 This is the beginning of several visions Jeremiah will be given as he delivers God's message at this time. The Almond was among the first trees to wake up in the Spring. It had flowers clearly before other trees. Judah had been acting as if God is asleep. The message of the almond is," God is awake. The God of the universe does not sleep. He is 'up early'".

vv.13-16 Here we have the first warnings of an upcoming Babylonian invasion. The reason God is allowing this evil people to overthrow his chosen nation is given in v.16.

vv.17,18 The time has come to get to work. It is now time to stand up and be counted. God will establish him. Verse 18 lists some pictures of God's strength and protection.

v.19 God promises Jeremiah to support and protect him. The enemies would not prevail against Jeremiah because God was with him.

Chapter 2

vv.1-3 This chapter begins with reference back to a time of great faithfulness. This was a time when Israel was dependent upon God. God had chosen them to be his own special nation. He was their provider and protector and they looked to him only.

v.4 Listen up. This is God's message. Here are God's accusations.

v.5 What charge can be brought against God that would explain Israel's rejection?

vv.6,7 Through the generations God has blessed and provided for this people, but now they no longer seek out the God who has blessed them in the past. Instead they are taking the blessings for granted and are rejecting the God who has provided for them.

v.8 Priest and prophet have forgotten the laws of God (discovery of law by Hilkiah). Prophecies have come to be made by Baal. The people have taken to chasing idols who cannot help them.

v.9 God does not hold this people blameless. (See **Ex. 20:4-7**)

vv.10,11 Look at the practices of the heathen peoples. None of them would even consider changing gods and their gods are not gods. Israel had exchanged the God of Glory for profitless idols.

v.12 This is astonishing. It should cause terror.

v.13 What Israel has done would be like turning away from a constant running spring of fresh water and choosing rather to drink from a stagnant, leaky cistern (a place where there was not always the assurance of water).

vv.14-17 These were freeborn people who through their rejection of the God who had selected and blessed them have brought oppression and slavery upon themselves.

vv.18,19 Israel has had a long-standing tradition of going to Egypt and Assyria and making alliances with them rather than trusting God to deliver them. The message here is clear. They will pay for their failure to seek out and trust in God.

v.20 It was God who had constantly delivered them and given them freedom -- yet Israel sought other lovers (gods). They committed spiritual adultery. They played the harlot under every green tree. (The mention of the green trees could have reference to the worship of the Asherah.)

v.21 By prostituting themselves in this way they were taking the noble, upright purpose of God and were making it profane and degenerate.

v.22 They could not wash away their iniquity. They could not hide their sin.

vv.23-25 No matter how much they denied their rejection of God, they had polluted themselves. The kings between Hezekiah and Josiah brought in all kinds of wickedness. They had broken loose like a runaway camel. They were like a wild donkey in heat giving themselves to false gods. By their actions they were saying, "I will go in my own way and do as I choose." Theirs was a refusal to be controlled.

vv.26-28 They should be ashamed for turning to gods of wood and stone which could not possibly save them. This idolatry was so widespread every city had their own gods.

vv.29,30 God says why plead with me? (See **Judges 6:7-10**) You have transgressed. You have refused my discipline and chastening. You have killed the prophets I have sent to warn you and bring you back. {Jesus' lament in **Matt. 23:37**}

v.31 This is a picture of childish foolishness in rejecting the source of their strength to "do it myself".

v.32 A bride does not forget the beauty and joy of her wedding day, yet God is accusing Israel of forgetting their betrothal to God and going after false lovers.

vv.33,34 Again we have the picture of spiritual prostitution. Judah had become so wicked it was as if they were teaching wickedness to the wicked. They had the blood of the innocents on their skirts.{Atrocities of Manasseh and Amon **2 Kings 21:2-9; 19-22**}

v.35 In spite of all of this there was still the claim of innocence.

vv.36,37 They were gadding about; running from one false help to another. All these weak earthly alliances will do is lead them into slavery.

NOTES

Chapter 3

v.1 This chapter begins with a reminder of God's divorce law that if a man put his wife away and she married another he could not remarry her if she became single again through divorce or widowhood. (**Deut. 24:1-4**) If he did, God had said it would be a pollution of the land. What Israel and Judah were doing was worse. They kept going back and forth between lovers spiritually, This is what Elijah referred to as halting between two opinions. They were fence sitting; trying to take the best from all lovers.

v.2 Israel had polluted the land with her harlotries. Like the Arabian she was lying in wait to ambush or go after false gods. Reading through the historical books we read constantly of the high places. Idol worship took place on these high places (high hills). {The thought was the higher you built your temple or altar the closer you would be to the gods thus at an advantage.}

v.3 As punishment God had withheld rains to get unfaithful Israel's attention. This goes back to the promises of blessing and cursing in **Lev. 26**. Somehow the message was not getting through to this wicked people.

vv.4,5 Israel called to God to stop the punishment but were unwilling to stop sinning. There was no repentance.

v.6 During the reign of Josiah the king had called the people to come back to God and serve him. Add to this they had the example of the punishment God had brought on the Northern kingdom.

v.7 Judah had seen God's patience with Israel and how God dealt with them sending prophets to call them back.

v.8 Finally he had to put her away - cast her off - cut his ties to her - divorce. God gave Israel over to the Assyrians. Judah did not get the message.

v.9 Stones and trees have reference to the idolatry practiced by Israel.

v.10 Judah's turning back to God was only half-hearted. They were going back and forth between God and the false idols.

v.11 Israel had not been as hypocritical. After the division of the kingdom their history was one of constant idolatry.

vv.12,13 Jeremiah was told to call to Northern Israel and offer God's mercy and forgiveness if they will admit their wickedness and repent.

v.14 This has reference to a remnant from Israel that will be faithful and come to the Lord.

v.15 To those who return God promises faithful leaders.

vv.16,17 The ark will no longer be God's throne. All of Jerusalem (spiritual kingdom) will be God's throne. [All in the church will come before God] The ark may have already been gone, there is definitely no mention of it after Babylonian captivity. God cannot be contained by boxes or temples made with hands. (Acts **17:24-27**)

v.18 The picture of one nation once again is either a reference to the fact that there will only be one Jewish nation following the Babylonian captivity, or is a prophecy of the Church where all may enter and be one. (**Eph. 2:14-18**)

v.19 God has always desired to be a loving, blessing father to his children. He has wanted to give what is best. This blessing was for the non-rebellious.

v.20 It was Israel that turned away, not God. They had deserted him not he them.

v.21 This seems to be a reference to Godly sorrow which must precede true repentance. **(2 Cor. 7: 10)**

v.22 God's offered forgiveness.

vv.23-25 Here we have a confession of guilt and foolishness. This is also a part of repentance.

NOTES

Chapter 4

vv.1-4 *A Call to Repentance*

v.1 God in calling for Israel to repent tells them that such a return will require a whole-hearted effort on their part. They must put away all of the detestable things, the abominations connected to their idolatry.

v.2 They then must demonstrate a total dependence upon God. Their dependence should be so complete that the nations looking on will have no doubt about their devotion. The nations would be blessed by Israel's commitment.

vv.3,4 Go to work. Clean out the trash of your former life. Put away all of your idols. Break up your hardened heart. Fully prepare yourselves and devote yourselves to serving God. This must be done or they will know the wrath of God!

vv.5-18 *Disaster from the North*

In these verses Jeremiah is directed to once again give warning about an imminent Babylonian invasion and what that will entail.

v.5 Run to the fortified cities, cities with walls.

v.6 Call for all to flee to safety for disaster is coming from the North (Babylon).

v.7 Nebuchadnezzar will be as vicious as a lion attacking from the thicket. As the lion destroys men so Babylon will destroy nations. Lands and cities will be wasted.

v.8 The advice is to put on sackcloth, to lament and wail. As you may remember when Jonah warned Nineveh of God's imminent wrath this is what they did to demonstrate their humble repentance and fear. On that occasion God's fierce anger was turned.

v.9 Courage will desert the leaders of Israel. They will view the coming destruction with amazement. They will not believe that it is actually coming as we will see as we continue this study.

v.10 This coming disaster will be so astonishing because all along God has been viewed as the God of peace. When he brings this sure destruction God will be accused of deception. This does not fit the picture Jeremiah and others have had of God.

vv.11,12 Babylon will come through the land like a wind of destruction wiping out everything.

v.13 This thought continues with the pictures of clouds, whirlwinds, and fast eagles. Babylon will strike as quickly as lightening and will be as destructive as a tornado.

v.14 In light of this Jeremiah once again calls for Israel to repent while there is still time.

v.15 Dan and Mt. Ephraim were in the far North of Israel. As such they would be the first to see the approaching armies of Babylon.

vv.16,17 Send out the warning. God is bringing this calamity on the cities of Israel.

v.18 The message to Israel is, "You have brought this on yourself. When you rejected God, he removed his blessings from you. He is giving you what you wanted."

vv.19-31 *Anguish over Judah's Destruction*

v.19 Because of this vision of things to come Jeremiah is pained to the core.

v.20 The whole land will be plundered. Everyone will be touched. (Reference to his own tents and curtains.)

v.21 Rank upon rank they keep coming.

v.22 The people are foolish for not knowing God and obeying his commands. It has come to the point that all they know to do is evil. They have forgotten the good. When men know not God, disaster is sure. (**2 Thes. 1:7-9**)

vv.23-26 The devastation will be complete. Everything will be destroyed. All the greatness God has given will be taken away. It will seem that they will be going back to the time before the creation of life.

v.27 This is a note of hope in the midst of the anguish. There is the hope of restoration.

v.28 Even so this devastating destruction is sure. It is going to happen.

v.29 All men will run for their lives.

v.30 God says that at that time it will be useless to try to attract their false lovers (dress like the harlot). Your lovers will despise you - There will be no deliverance except from God.

v.31 There will be the cry of anguish and pain as the nation falls to the destroyers. This will be the sound of Jerusalem in her death throes.

NOTES

Chapter 5

v.1 The level of depravity and rejection of God was so complete that Jeremiah could not find one righteous man so that Jerusalem might be saved. This is reminiscent of Abrahams bargaining with God over the city of Sodom only this time we are talking about the city where God had put his name and none could be found faithful to him.

v.2 There was still the claim of being God's people but it was a lie. {Much like a nation calling itself a Christian nation but rejecting all association with God.}

v.3 God had tried to bring them back through gentle loving discipline but they had hardened their hearts and stiffened their necks in their rejection of him and his will.

vv.4,5 Jeremiah at first thought that this rejection was just among the poor, ignorant, lower classes but when he searched out the great he found that they were just as wicked even though they should have known better.

v.6 Because of their rejection of God they are marked for destruction. No matter where they turn, forest, desert, or city, they cannot escape.

vv.7-9 God had fed and blessed and Israel accepted the blessings then went after other gods. They were well fed at home but still lusted after the other. [This may be some reference to the prostitution rites of Caananitish religion also.] The grass looked greener elsewhere. This attitude was sure to bring God's punishment.

v.10 There is a ray of hope here. Judah will not be brought to a complete end.

vv.11-13 The attitude had become, "we can do whatever we want because God is a loving, blessing God and won't really destroy us." The prophets had become just wind bags with no substance and no truth. {We hear similar lies in the religious world when we are told that a loving God will never condemn anyone.}

v.14 Jeremiah's message would be one of punishment as fire that consumes wood.

vv.15-17 A mighty nation is coming. It will be a nation of foreigners (Daniel's training). It will be an army of mighty men with death in their quivers. This nation will wipe you out. Your fortified cities will not help.

v.18. Still there will not be a complete annihilation. A remnant will remain to be captive in Babylon.

v.19 Because Israel had forsaken God for foreign gods, God will give them up to serve in foreign lands.

vv.20,21 This message is for all of Israel. Listen up! Pay attention!

v.22 A recognition of God's great power was needed here. This is the God who kept the sea at bay. {This could be a reference back to the flood. God had the power to turn it all loose again. See **2 Pet. 3:5-7**}

v.23-25 Instead we see a refusal to recognize the goodness and control and power of God. It was iniquity that brought this punishment on this people.

vv.26-29 The rejection of God led to selfish, uncaring behavior (atheism, no moral law, might makes right). So, the attitude was get to the top anyway you can . You don't have time for anyone but self.

vv.30,31 This had led to an appalling situation. The prophets were false prophets and the priests were ruling by their own authority instead of the authority of God, and the people approved. The message is the end is coming and who will you who have rejected God turn to?

Chapter 6

v.1 Flee, disaster is coming. This is a personal call as Jeremiah was from Benjamin.

v.2 The beautiful Jerusalem, the city special to God, the city where God had placed his name will be destroyed.

v.3 Even this beautiful pasture will be wiped out as a pasture in which sheep are allowed to stay and over pasture. Sheep are notorious for wiping out a pasture if they are not kept moving. The destruction here will be as complete as sheep that are not moved.

vv.4,5 The attacks will seem endless. They will come day and night and it is much harder to defend or even escape in the dark.

vv.6,7 God is directing this attack, calling for this punishment. God is calling for this because of the oppression Israel had demonstrated. Their wickedness was as overflowing as water from a natural spring.

v.8 Take warning lest you be made a desolate, uninhabited land (wiped out).

v.9 The coming destruction will be complete. Gleaners stripped the vines of what had been left by the harvesters.

v.10 This verse points to some of Jeremiah's frustration. Those whom he is warning will not listen and are not interested in God's message to them.

v.11a Jeremiah was full of God's message of wrath and could not hold it back.

vv.11b,12 God says let them have it. Everyone will be affected. Young, old, men, women, all will be defeated and taken. Their possessions will go to others (spoils of war?).

v.13 Again a reason for God's wrath. Israel was a greedy, covetous people and their leaders were liars.

v.14 (The lie.) Peace, peace. {God will keep us from being destroyed by war. This is just a temporary discomfort. Nothing really bad is going to happen.} (Truth.) There is no peace. This comfort is as useless as a Band-Aid on a gushing wound.

v.15 Israel was not ashamed of their wickedness. They were so used to their practices they could no longer blush.

v.16 This is a call to repentance. Go back to where you got off track. Seek the path of God where there is rest and blessing. The answer was NO!

v.17 The habit had become to reject the warnings from God's watchmen (prophets). People often killed the bearer of bad news. (**Matt. 23:37**)

vv.18,19 An explanation to the nations observing. God is bringing this punishment because of Israel's refusal to listen to God and their rejection of him. God was rejecting them for rejecting Him.

v.20 The problem cannot be solved by more offerings. Offering that is not accompanied by a contrite heart is useless. (**Psalm 51:16,17**)

v.21 All will be brought down!

vv.22-26 *The Terror of the Approaching Disaster*

vv.22,23 The people coming from the North are a cruel people. They show no mercy.

v.24 The report overwhelms with fear. They will be too weak to face this onslaught.

v.25 The onslaught will seem to come from everywhere. There will be no place to turn and avoid it. No escape.

v.26 Repent in sack cloth and ashes. Mourn over your sin as for the loss of a child. Lament over your sin.

vv.27-30 *The Picture of the Refiner*

v.27 The refiners job was to burn the impurities out of soft metals like silver and gold to make them pure and precious.

v.28 Israel had hardened themselves like bronze and iron. They were refusing to give up their impurities; refusing to be refined.

v.30 As such they are rejected.

NOTES

Chapter 7

vv.1-4 In this chapter we see worship abuses and the using of the temple as an indication of God's favor. Jeremiah tells them that they are guilty of false thinking. For this reason they need to repent or amend their ways. If they want to continue to enjoy God's favor in the promised land, they will have to repent.

vv.5-7 Jeremiah gives a listing of the kinds of things Judah will have to do in order to enjoy God's favor. This is evidence of repentance. John the Baptist preached a similar message in **Luke 3:7-14**.

v.8 They had been deceived by lying messengers.

vv.9,10 Verse 9 begins with a rhetorical question. Clearly Jeremiah is accusing them of doing all these things. Here we have a picture of worship abuse. They were practicing their idolatry then running to the temple to burn a little sacrifice thinking that this would solve all their problems. As long as the temple stood, this people thought they were fine.

v.11 The temple had been turned into a den of robbers in that the people were stealing that which should be God's and giving it to idols.

v.12 God says look what I did to Shiloh. Shiloh was the place the Tabernacle of God stood when Israel first came into the land of Canaan. In this instance it represents the Northern kingdom.

vv.13-15 The same judgment from God will come to Judah as he brought on Israel.

v.16 God tells Jeremiah to stop praying for Israel until they repent. (See **1 John 5:16**)

vv.17-19 Whole families were involved in idolatrous practices. In doing this they were provoking God's anger and bringing shame upon themselves.

v.20 God's wrath is about to be poured out and it will not be stopped.

vv.21,22 For all the good their burnt offerings were doing they might as well have been eating them themselves. Without repentance the sacrifice was useless.

v.23 God has required obedience more than sacrifice. The sacrifice was to be a part of the life of obedience and not a substitute for it. (See **1 Sam. 15:22** & **Psa. 51:16,17**)

v.24 This people was refusing to listen to the commands of God and in essence were walking backward (away from God) and not forward.

v.25 Since leaving Egypt God had constantly sent his messengers and prophets to this people to call them back to him and warn them against disobedience.

vv.26,27 Israel had made a habit of stubborn refusal to hear these prophets and repent, and this group was the worst yet. God is telling Jeremiah that he will not be heard.

v.28 They had become the nation that refused God.

v.29 In truth they had broken their Nazarite vow of devotion to God. When the Nazarite vow was broken or came to an end the hair was shaved off and thrown into the fire. This people should sing their lament or funeral dirge for God has abandoned them.

vv.30-34 *The Valley of Slaughter*

v.30 They were guilty of setting up detestable things (like pagan altars) in the temple itself.

v.31 They had built high places and pagan altars in Tophet (the valley of Hinnom). This is where they were offering their children to Molech.

vv.32-34 God says the day of destruction is coming when this place of worship will be changed to a burial ground where the dead bodies of the inhabitants of Jerusalem will be mounded up and left to rot. There will be so many corpses that no one will be left to chase off the carrion birds. The city will be silent. Celebrations will cease as there will be no cause for joy.

NOTES

Chapter 8

vv.1-3 When the Babylonian hordes attack they will also desecrate the tombs and graves. Bodies and bones will be brought out and scattered on the ground and left to rot like garbage [exposed to sun, moon and stars they had been worshipping]. Life will be so hard that death will be preferable to life.

v.4 Normally things go in cycles. Normally when men fall they get up again. When they make a wrong turn they go back to where they got off course and make correction.

v.5 Judah is breaking that cycle. They are refusing to return, choosing to continue in their apostasy.

v.6 There has been no remorse, no repentance, instead they are rushing headlong into wickedness like horses rushing into battle.

v.7 All creatures understand God's plan for them. Not so this people or if they understand it they are rejecting it.

v.8 Their actions contradict their statements. The lying pen of the scribe has given them false security.

v.9 The so-called wise are being put to shame for they have gone after false wisdom and rejected God.

v.10 All which they have gone after greedily through their covetousness will be taken from them and given to others.

vv.11,12 Here we have a repeat of the message of 6:14,15. The false teachers are giving a false hope. Unfortunately where there has been no shame, and no repentance, there will be no rescue.

v.13 This goes back to the picture of annihilation presented earlier in the book.

v.14 The destruction is sure. Even going to fortified cities will not spare them.

v.15 No peace or good is coming.

vv.16,17 Here again we have a picture of a thunderous attack from the North. So large an army the earth shakes. The serpents in these verses are representing this attacking, killing force.

v.18 This verse begins a section of remorse or mourning on the part of Jeremiah which will continue into the next chapter. The prophet is seriously saddened.

v.19 God, while still present in Zion, is not rescuing this people at this time because they have rejected him and provoked him through their idolatry.

v.20 This truly is a hopeless cry. This people have had their chance to repent and be reconciled to God but now it is too late.

v.21 Jeremiah is in great sorrow over the needless fate of his people.

v.22 Where then can they go for healing. By refusing to turn back to God and be faithful to him they have rejected the only source of true healing. (See **Heb. 10:26-31**)

Chapter 9

v.1 Jeremiah continues to mourn over lost Israel. The loss is so great he prays for an abundant supply of tears.

v.2 The people remain treacherous and unfaithful to God in spite of Jeremiah's warnings. So we see him wanting to escape, run away to some secluded haven of rest.

vv.3-9 *The Lord's Answer to Jeremiah*

v.3 Destructive lies are now the pattern of the people. They shoot off deceit like an archer his arrows. They have achieved power through dishonesty. And they have so rejected God that he says of them, "they do not know me."

vv.4-6 The deceit has become so commonplace that you cannot trust anyone. Everyone is out for himself and God's way is rejected. The land has become a land of deceit that refuses to acknowledge God.

v.7 God promises to put them through a purifying furnace. Things are going to get hot as God burns away their impurity.

v.8 The deadly lies are abusive. They would say one thing to a neighbor (peace) while at the same time plotting against him.

v.9 These habits, this hypocrisy, will bring punishment and vengeance from God. God has always promised to avenge the abused and downtrodden. [Look at **Luke 18:7,8; Romans 12:19;** and **Heb. 10:30**]

v.10 The land will be ravaged. Even the beasts will leave it (animals have an uncanny sense of when disaster is imminent and often run away).

v.11 Jerusalem will be turned into a wasteland.

vv.12-16 *An Explanation as to Why the Land will be Destroyed*

v.12 The answer is one which seems to have escaped even the wisest.

v.13 This people has forsaken God, they were not obedient to his will nor have they walked in his way. (See **1 John 1:5,6**)

v.14 They have chosen rather to follow the Baals.

v.15 As a result God will feed them bitterness and death.

v.16 God will scatter them among foreign nations and they will fall to foreign soldiers.

vv.17-23 *The Call for the Mourners*

v.17 It is time to call in the funeral mourners for death is at hand.

v.18 Lament and mourn and weep (**James 4:9**).

v.19 The wail that will go up from Jerusalem is, "we are plundered for we have forsaken the Lord. We are driven from our homes."

v.20 God tells them to learn well the funeral dirge and teach it to their children for their punishment will not be temporary.

v.21 Death has come to all of the nation. Not even the children and the young will be spared. {This is much like the death of the first born in Egypt.}

v.22 The land will be scattered with dead bodies because there will be no one to retrieve them. They will be like grain stalks or manure on the ground left to lie and rot.

v.23 Don't brag about your wisdom, your riches or your might [everything comes from God].

v.24 If you must boast, boast that you know God who shows lovingkindness and righteousness. Brag that you have the sense to follow God. This is pretty much what Paul said to the Corinthians and others.

vv.25,26 The day is coming when circumcised Israel will be punished just like the un-circumcised Gentile nations around them who have rejected God. Circumcision was the mark of the covenant between God and Israel. When they rejected God they might as well have been un-circumcised for the covenant was broken. Israel was not the only nation overrun by Babylon.

NOTES

Chapter 10

This chapter falls rather naturally into two sections. The first section is a contrast between the true God and the idols being worshipped. This may have also been a warning against worshipping the idols of the land during their upcoming captivity. The second section pictures the total destruction of the nation by God through the use of Babylon.

vv.1-16 *The Wisdom of Following God*

v.1 The Lord is calling to the people to listen to him. In this way he is calling them back from idolatry.

v.2 The message is don't follow the customs of the nations. Don't follow astrology (signs in the heavens).

vv.3-5 Idol worship is useless folly. Men cut and shape the tree to become the idol. They adorn it with gold and silver and prop it up so it will stand and not fall over. Even then it is more like a scarecrow in a cucumber patch than a god. It can do nothing for itself. Why worship an idol that you made and that can do nothing for you?

vv.6,7 God on the other hand is unique. There is none like him. As such he is deserving of honor and respect among the wise of all nations.

vv.8,9 Idols are worthless and only fools would worship them. They are designed, carved, shaped, and dressed by men.

v.10 God is the true God. He has control over all of creation. At his voice the earth quakes. Nations cannot endure his wrath. [He establishes nations and he brings them down.]

v.11 Powerless idols will be destroyed.

vv.12,13 God created all things and controls all things including the weather. He sends the wind and rain. He makes the lightening.

vv.14,15 Idols are works of foolishness. They will disappoint all who trust in them. In due time they will be destroyed.

v.16 God is not like these. He is the Lord of Hosts, all-powerful, and He chose Israel to be his own.

vv.17-25 *The Punishment from God*

v.17 Gather up your possessions - you are overthrown.

v.18 God is going to sling you out of the land (evict?). He will bring distress on you and you will be captured.

v.19 The wound is grievous but must be endured.

v.20 Homes and children are gone and no one is left to help find or build shelter.

v.21 Because the leaders (shepherds) refused to seek the Lord's way the people are scattered.

v.22 Rumblings come from the North. The invading army will turn the land into an area suitable only for Jackals.

v.23 Man cannot direct his own life. When he does it leads to ruin.

vv.24,25 This is a prayer of Jeremiah. Correct me but not in your anger lest I be destroyed. Punish the nations who consume Jacob and lay her land waste. [God will indeed punish the punisher in his time.]

Chapter 11

This chapter begins with a reminder of Israel's covenant with God.

vv.1-3 Hear again the covenant. You need to be reminded of your contract with God. Part of that agreement is the one who does not obey will be cursed.

v.4 This covenant goes all the way back to their deliverance from cruel bondage in Egypt by God. (Life so hard it is called the iron furnace or iron smelter.) The promise from God was, "obey me and I will be your God and you shall be my people." Surely God's people are people of privilege.

v.5 God promised a land of blessing, a land flowing with milk and honey. (God kept this promise. He delivered on his side of the contract.)

v.6 Jeremiah was to keep reminding Judah of their agreement. Tell them to do what they promised. Hold up their end of the bargain.

v.7 God had continually called for Israel to come back to him. He had sent prophet after prophet for this purpose and the message was always "obey my voice".

v.8 They constantly refused to obey so now they will suffer the curses that were a part of the covenant.

v.9 It is as if they had entered a conspiracy to plot against God.

v.10 The people have gone back into the iniquity of their fathers by practicing idolatry. During the reign of Josiah there had been a restoration of obedience to God but now that Josiah is gone the old wickedness has returned. They have broken the covenant.

v.11 As a result God says I will bring inescapable calamity against them and will not hear their cries. [During the time of the Judges God had always heard the cries of distress and raised up a deliverer. This time there will be no deliverer.]

v.12 They can cry out to their false gods but it will do them no good for gods created by men are unable to help anyone.

v.13 Things have degenerated to the point that this people have as many gods as they have villages and streets in their cities.

v.14 Jeremiah is told once again not to pray for this people for their destruction was sure and unavoidable.

v.15 They were doing lewd things in the temple (idol worship) thinking God can be appeased with a little sacrifice. God says the sacrifices will not protect them. The party is over.

v.16 They had been bountifully blessed. They had been as beautiful and rich as a Green Olive tree full of fruit. Now they are destined for destruction and ugliness as a wind-broken burned out tree.

v.17 The very God who had established them as a nation has now pronounced doom against this people. They had brought this evil upon themselves. They were to blame for their failure. They had constantly provoked God's anger with their idolatry; the worship of Baal.

vv.18,19 God reveals to Jeremiah the plot to kill him. Jeremiah had been naive and blind to the plot against him.

v.20 Jeremiah was totally dependent upon God. He is trusting God to protect and avenge.

vv.21-23 This plot was coming from Anathoth, Jeremiah's home town, a town approximately three miles from Jerusalem. They have demanded that Jeremiah cease his prophesying (See **Acts 5:28,29**) The message from Anathoth was, "quit or die." God said that he would punish them and they would be destroyed.

Chapter 12

vv.1-4 *In Jeremiah's Distress that His Own People Will Seek His Life He Begins this Section with Questions to God.*

v.1 How can you in your righteousness and justice allow these people to succeed? [Tempted and tried.]

v.2 You have established them and blessed them and even though they may praise you they do not mean it. You are not high on their list of priorities. They are only paying lip service. [This is the same message Isaiah spoke in **Isa. 29:13** and Jesus quoted in **Matt. 15:8**. God knew that this would be the direction many would take.]

v.3 Jeremiah is saying God you know me inside and out like David in **Ps. 139**. He says you have put me to the test. Punish these wicked ones.

v.4 How long will the land suffer the consequences of the sin of this people? They are saying God does not see or care what we do or Jeremiah will not live to see what happens to us.

vv.5,6 Here We Have the Beginning of God's Answer. Things have not gotten hard yet. The situation will get harder. It will come to the point where even your family will turn against you and you will only be able to depend on God.

vv.7-13 *Promise of Punishment*

v.7 I have turned my beloved over to her enemies.

v.8 Because my heritage roared against me I have hated (turned away my love) them.

v.9 Now they will be like a vulture attacked by vultures. Bring all the animals into the attack.

v.10 The rulers (shepherds, pastors) are to blame. They have brought this destruction and caused this desolation.

v.11 No one cares.

v.12 The destroyers have come. No one is safe. [The message is sin will be punished.]

v.13 Because of wickedness they will feel the fierce anger of the Lord and life will be hard [plant wheat and reap thorns. This, the promised consequence of breaking the covenant and reminiscent of Adam's curse for his rebellion.]

vv.14-17 *A Promise of Restoration*

v.14 God's punishment against the oppressors is promised. Israel will be plucked from their hands.

v.15 Israel will be brought back and reestablished in the land.

v.16 For this to happen the people must turn back to God. They must be taught to trust the Lord as fully as they had previously trusted the Baals. [This verse also seems to include a prophesy of the eventual conversion and inclusion of Gentiles into God's covenant]

v.17 Even so in the midst of this message of hope is the stern reminder that if they do not obey they will face utter destruction.

Chapter 13

vv.1-11 *The Linen Sash, (Belt, Waistband, Loincloth, Shorts). This is an Illustration lesson. The Glory of the Jews Will be Marred by Captivity in Babylon.*

v.1 Jeremiah is told to take a new linen sash and wear it, but it is not to be washed. (This is representative of the uncleanness of the Jews.)

v.2 Jeremiah carries out this order.

vv.3,4 He is then told to hide the sash in the rocks by the Euphrates. (The taking of Israel into captivity.)

v.5 Again Jeremiah follows his instructions.

v.6 After some time passes, Jeremiah is told to retrieve the sash.

v.7 When Jeremiah brought the sash back it was ruined. (Israel would never again know the glory and prominence they had had prior to Babylonian captivity.)

vv.8,9 In this way God will ruin the pride of Judah.

v.10 Evil, pride filled Judah, because they had practiced selfishness and idolatry, will be rendered worthless like the sash.

v.11 God had intended to keep them close to himself but they refused and so are destined to be ruined by Babylon.

vv.12-14 *The Wine Bottle Lesson*

v.12 Every bottle will be filled with wine. (The reply of Israel is "that's obvious".)

38 | Jeremiah

v.13 Here we have the explanation of the wine bottle allusion. Every vessel (body, life) will be filled with drunkenness (foolishness). The worst offenders will be the leaders who have operated so foolishly in leading the people.

v.14 As a result God will dash them together. There will be no pity. No mercy. All will be destroyed.

vv.15-27 *The Promise of Captivity*

vv.15,16 Hear the Lord, obey him. Repent before you are caused to wander in darkness.

v.17 If you will not hear God I will weep for you for your punishment is sure.

vv.18,19 To the Queen and King. You have no place to run. You will be brought down and your whole land will be captive.

v.20 In reference to the failure of these leaders the question is asked where are your sheep that you were supposed to be tending? (See **John 10.11-13**)

v.21 Where are your allies? They are the ones attacking you.

v.22 Why are you being embarrassed like this? It is the reward for your iniquity.

v.23 They had behaved in this way for so long there was no more hope of their changing than a leopard changing his spots or a black man changing his skin.

v.24 As a result you will be scattered like dust in the wind.

vv.25-27 You trusted in falsehood now I will show you up for the harlot you are. Woe to you, will you not be made clean? They could have been made clean by turning back to God.

Chapter 14

vv.1-6 *Description of Famine Conditions*

v.2 This is the description of a natural reaction to a long lasting famine condition.

v.3 This famine was affecting all levels of society. The nobles are sending their servants to the cisterns and other places water could normally be found only to have them return in shame for there is no water to be found.

v.4 The farmers see the parched land and despair for there is not enough moisture to plant their crops. [One year my grandfather experienced such a dry summer that he knew his beans would not produce enough to take the combine to the field. He went in with his disk and turned the whole crop under. I remember him commenting that that was some expensive fertilizer.]

v.5 This famine is so great the deer were deserting their young to hunt for grass.

v.6 The wild donkeys are blind and have to sniff the air for any scent of food. There is none.

vv.7-9 *A Prayer for Forgiveness and Help*

v.7 This is a repeat of the regular pattern of Israel. Throughout the book of Judges we would see rebellion followed by punishment then there would be a confession of sin and a temporary faithfulness. Over and over this pattern has been repeated. Here we see the prayer of confession seeking that God's favor be restored.

v.8 This verse almost makes it seem that God is to blame for their hardship at this time. God you are the hope of Israel why are you acting like a stranger. Why are you separating yourself from us? {Have you ever said "Don't be a stranger" to a friend as they were leaving your house? You were saying don't stay away. Come often. Weren't you?} Here Israel is asking, "God why are you making yourself a stranger?" They had answered their own question.

v.9 You are our God. You can save. Why are you acting like one who is confused about what to do? (See **Isa. 59:1,2**)

vv.10-12 *God's Answer*

v.10 You love wandering too much. You practice no self-restraint. Therefore, God has rejected you.

v.11 Once again Jeremiah is told not to pray for this people. (They would not repent.)

v.12 Simply going through the motions of ritual devotion to God is not going to save them. Their judgment is sure. (To be saved there must be the penitent contrite heart as David said in **Psalm 51**.)

v.13 Here we have the lie of the false prophets that the people were clinging to. {This is that same message of peace when there was no peace. They had the people convinced that God was not really going to punish them and destroy them. (It almost sounds like the same message that a loving, merciful God would never condemn anyone to an eternal hell that we are hearing from so many groups today.)}

vv.14-16 *God's Answer About the Lying Prophets*

v.14 These false prophets are lying. They are claiming to be God's messengers and to be speaking for God when they are not.

vv.15,16 God said these false messengers will suffer the very fate they are saying God is not going to bring. And sadly their followers, those who have believed their false message will die right along with them. Their bodies will be thrown out into the streets and there will be no one to bury them.

vv.17-19 *The Lament of Jeremiah*

v.17 The prophet is weeping over the judgment this people have brought on themselves as well as for the innocent who will suffer along with them. (God's messenger is always distressed over the loss of a single soul. We must never appear to be happy that men and women are going to hell.)

v.18 Everywhere he turns there is death and devastation. In the country he sees the bodies of the slain. In the city are those killed by famine and disease. And prophet and priest are taken into captivity.

v.19 Judah is rejected. There is no healing. There is no peace.

vv.20-22 *A Prayer of Confession and Hope by the Prophet*

v.20 Here Jeremiah is confessing the iniquity of his people.

v.21 Then there is the petition for forgiveness and a renewal of the covenant. [Begging for another chance.]

v.22 Finally there is the confession of the majesty, power, authority, and magnificence of almighty God.

NOTES

Chapter 15

v.1 Even if Moses and Samuel joined in with Jeremiah in prayers of supplication for Israel it would not change God's mind concerning his punishment of this idolatrous people at this point. Israel had broken the covenant, so God was casting them away.

v.2 There seems to be a slight play on words in this verse. As God has cast Israel away the question arises, "Where shall we go?" The answer from God is those destined for death will go to death, those for the sword to the sword, those destined for famine will go to famine and those destined for captivity will go to captivity.

v.3 God says they will be destroyed four ways: The sword will slay. Dogs will drag off the slain. Birds will feed on the slain bodies. And beasts will clean the bones.

v.4 The southern kingdom will be handed over to trouble from foreign countries because of the wickedness of Manasseh. {To learn the wicked leadership of Manasseh turn to **2 Kings 21**. Verses 1-7 list some of the atrocities committed by this king who was the son of Hezekiah. Verse 16 adds to the list. God's prophecy against Judah as the result of this kings atrocities is recorded in **2 Kings 21:10-15**.} As you can see Jeremiah's message should not have been a surprise because it had been promised by God years earlier.

v.5 This is a rhetorical question. The message is clear. No one will pity. There will be no sympathy. No one will care.

v.6 Judah had forsaken God. God says they have gone backward (away from God). As a result God will destroy them. The days of patient forbearance are over.

v.7 Judah will be scattered like the chaff from the wheat. Families will be separated from each other. Men, women and children will be killed.

v.8 There will be an abundance of widows. The plunder will come at noonday. Anguish and terror are their lot.

v.9 Mourn for whole families. All will be given over to the enemies, God is no longer their protector and champion.

vv.10-18 *Contain a Series of Dialogs Between Jeremiah and God*

v.10 As you can imagine Jeremiah is dejected and depressed upon having to constantly deliver such a negative message. Here he expresses a wish that he had never been born. He is all alone. The king has rejected his message. The people curse him. His own family is plotting to kill him. Every direction he turns there just seems to be more trouble.

v.11 God promises Jeremiah protection. He says that the enemy will take care of him; protect him.

vv.12-14 In these verses God once again tells what is to happen. Judah will be unable to defeat this enemy. Going against them will be like trying to break iron and bronze. As a result of their defeat their treasures will be taken away. All of this is due to the wide spread sin in the nation. So they will be taken captive and made slaves in a foreign land. This is going to happen. God's anger cannot be appeased or quenched.

v.15 Jeremiah is crying out for God's justice and vengeance. He has suffered for the sake of God.

v.16 Jeremiah's words were God's words. That was what God had promised when he called Jeremiah to take on this mission (**Jer. 1:9**). Jeremiah was God's man.

v.17 In this verse we see the loneliness of Jeremiah's devotion to God. He does not join in the revelry of the mockers. He is filled with

God's anger. [This may also be an allusion to the Blessed man of **Psalm 1.**]

v.18 This verse truly voices the despair of Jeremiah. "Why do I have this constant suffering?" He is so frustrated he even questions God's reliability to some extent. Will God disappoint like a dried up spring?

vv.19-21 *In These Verses We Find God's Reassurance to Jeremiah*

v.19 Come back to me, Don't be foolish. Be my prophet. Be my spokesman. You cannot give in to this people.

vv.20,21 In these verses we see once again God's promise of protection and deliverance to Jeremiah.

NOTES

Chapter 16

vv.1,2 Jeremiah, like many of the messengers of God is called upon to live his message. The devastation that is coming will be so great that it would be better to be unmarried and childless. Jeremiah is the only prophet we know of that was forbidden to marry. [I see an echo of this idea in Paul's teaching in **1 Corinthians 7** especially verse **26**.]

vv.3,4 God gives Jeremiah a reason to remain unmarried and childless. Men, women, and children will face gruesome deaths. Sword and famine will be no respecter of persons. Rotting bodies will stack up. (This is a picture of the awful atrocity of war.)

vv.5-7 Jeremiah is not to join in the mourning rituals either. God has removed his peace, loving kindness, and mercy from this people. (Jeremiah is to do nothing to try and lessen the pain.) This is also a message that funerals will cease because there will neither be time nor personnel to conduct them. The cutting of oneself for the dead was a heathen practice which was forbidden to the Israelites anyway. Again we see the picture of stacked up unburied bodies left to scavengers because there is no one to bury them and no one to mourn.

vv.8,9 Feasting and joyous celebrations will also cease. There will be nothing to celebrate. All occasions for mirth will have come to an end.

vv.10-13 This section begins with the cry of, "Why has God forsaken us?" God's answer is clear. "You have forsaken me. Your fathers did atrocious things and you have done worse. You have gone after evil ways. Because of this you will be cast out to a foreign land where you can worship your foreign gods because I will not show you favor."

vv.14,15 These verses present a bright spot through a promise of restoration. The time will come when God will be praised and remembered more for his deliverance from Babylon than he was for his deliverance from Egypt. This makes sense. What would be foremost on the minds of those delivered? It would be the more recent deliverance from Babylon.

v.16 Once again we have a reminder of how terrible and thorough this captivity will be. They will be dragged away with fishhooks and hunted out of every hiding place by their adversary.

v.17 God knows what has been going on. He knows their ways, their actions, even their thoughts.

v.18 Because of this God says they will pay double for their iniquity and sin. They will pay for their detestable idolatrous practices.

vv.19,20 God is a God of strength. He is a mighty fortress protecting those devoted to him. The nations (Gentiles) will see this and confess "what we have worshipped and served is not God."

v.21 They will see God's power and might and know he is the Lord.

{This seems to be a picture of God's mercy and grace being extended to all nations.}

Chapter 17

v.1 Sin and evil desire had been engraved deeply on the hearts of Israel. It had become an indelible part of their makeup. (The iron stylus was used to engrave on the hardest of substances.)

v.2 This people loved their idols like they loved their children. Generation after generation had been given over to the worship of idols. The situation was so bad that the children of that generation could remember only idol worship it had been so long since there had been worship of the true God. Idolatry was all they had seen in their homes. (What will our children remember about our attitude toward God and worship to him?)

v.3 Jerusalem will be destroyed and given over to her enemies.

v.4 Because of the iniquity of this people they will lose everything. God's bounty will be taken away from them. Captivity and slavery is sure. All because they have brought God's wrath down upon themselves.

vv.5-8 These verses present a contrast between trusting in man and trusting in God. Israel often made earthly alliances with nations like Egypt and Assyria when all along they had God's help at hand as a part of their covenant with God. This was what Hezekiah pointed out to the citizens of Jerusalem when the armies of Assyria were threatening. (**2 Chron. 32:8**) The contrast Jeremiah presents is the difference between a plant planted in parched salty soil where survival is impossible and a tree planted by water where survival is assured. The message is clear. Place your trust in God. {This is similar to the message of **Psalm 1**.}

vv.9,10 It is what comes out of the heart of a man that defiles. Motivation for all kinds of evil begins in the heart. God sees the hearts and minds and will judge accordingly. This was Jesus message in **Matthew 5:21,22,27,28**.

v.11 The thief and cheat will be revealed and will lose. (See **James 5:1-6**)

vv.12-18 *This Section Includes Jeremiah's Prayer for Protection and Deliverance*

vv.12,13 God is praised and recognized as the high king and sanctuary for Israel. He is their only hope. Those who forsake him will be ashamed. Their accomplishments will be written in the dust where it will blow away and be forgotten.

v.14 God is healer and savior.

v.15 This is a message of scoff and ridicule rejecting Jeremiah as God's spokesman.

v.16 Jeremiah prays, "God you know how faithful I have been."

vv.17,18 Deliver me, protect me, and avenge me of my enemies.

vv.19-23 These verses contain God's call that Israel return to Sabbath remembrance. Sabbath keeping was a part of loving God with one's whole being. God gave the Sabbath so that man might rest from his labors and remember the goodness of God. Sabbath failure was a symptom of complete rebellion against God. When men forsook the Sabbath they also forsook the God who gave the Sabbath. Sabbath failure was a sign of covetous greed (if I can work seven days a week I can make more money) and covetousness is idolatry. Unfortunately this people stiffened their necks and refused God's instruction (v.23).

vv.24-27 Obedience and recognition of God would bring renewed blessing and honor. Rejection of God would only bring destruction and disaster.

Chapter 18

vv.1-11 *The Lesson of the Pottery Shop*

vv.1,2 Jeremiah is told by God to go observe the potter so that he might deliver God's message. {Jeremiah did not just make an observation in life and decide that would make a good illustration and lesson. He was sent. This was God's message.}

vv.3,4 While at the potter's Jeremiah observes that the clay is completely under the potter's control. If one form does not work, the potter reshapes the clay to form another vessel.

vv.5,6 Israel is clay in God's hands. He has the power to shape and reshape.

vv.7-10 The direction God takes a nation is dependent upon that nation's faithfulness to him. Even nations marked for destruction can be spared by repentance. {See Nineveh in Jonah's day.} Likewise, blessed nations will be brought down by rebellion.

v.11 Judah is marked for disaster. Only repentance will spare them. (Once again there is the call to repent.)

v.12 Judah's response is, "It's too late. We like the life we are living too much to change. We are going to do what we want to do."

vv.13-17 *God's Response to Israel's Rebellion*

v.13 This is a senseless decision.

v.14 Men do not leave the well-watered fertile land of Lebanon's heights to take a farm on a piece of rock. Snow is always on top of Lebanon. Good springs of water do not just mysteriously disappear.

Judah's response to God is as unthinkable as the snow suddenly disappearing or the good stream suddenly drying up.

v.15 The description of Judah's senseless behavior continues. They have gone after idols instead of God. They have left good highways to follow cow paths.

v.16 The result of these ridiculous choices is the land will be left desolate. It will become a place the nations will be astonished at and reject. [This is just what God had promised.]

v.17 The people will be scattered. God will turn his back on them.

v.18 KILL THE MESSENGER. DISCREDIT HIM. SET TRAPS FOR HIM. WE DO NOT LIKE HIS MESSAGE.

vv.19-23 Jeremiah cries out to God in his rejection and despair. I have tried to do good by them and this is what I get in return. He is indignant and so cries: avenge me. Wipe them out. Don't forgive them, Let them cry out in pain. They have tried to bring me down so deal with them in your anger.

It is possible to love people and yet feel indignation for what they are doing.

Chapter 19

The Lesson of the Earthen jar

vv.1,2 Jeremiah is told to buy a ceramic flask or jar and then take it and some of the officials from Jerusalem out to Tophet or the Valley of Ben-Hinnom for a visual lesson.

v.3 Such a catastrophe is going to be brought through this valley by God that everyone who hears about it will have tingling ears. (It will seem to be unbelievable.)

vv.4,5 The reason for this coming disaster is explained. These people have set up their worship here in the garbage dump of the city. Idolatrous worship to unknown gods was practiced here. That idolatrous worship included human sacrifice. This is a practice which God would never have thought of asking for.

v.6 Because of all of this the valley will come to be known as the valley of slaughter. (So much human slaughter will take place in this area that slaughter will be what the area is known for.)

v.7 Wise council will disappear and as a result of God's defeating wise counsel there will come sure defeat. {God brought defeat to Absalom by defeating the counsel of his advisor, Ahithophel in **2 Sam. 17:14**}

v.8 The destruction of Jerusalem will be so complete that everyone who passes will shake their head and hiss. They will scorn and laugh at this once great city which now has become a place to be avoided.

v.9 During the siege the people of Jerusalem will be starving so much they will turn to cannibalism to survive.

vv.10,11 Jerusalem will be completely broken like the broken jar. They will be unmendable. They will never be the same again. Tophet will become the burying place until there is no more room to bury bodies.

vv.12,13 Beautiful Jerusalem will be turned into a garbage dump. All because of their idolatry and rejection of God.

vv.14,15 Jeremiah comes from Tophet back to the Temple court and declares God's judgment. Doom is coming because the people have become stubborn in their refusal to heed God's warnings.

Chapter 20

vv1,2 Pashhur, a priest and official in the temple, in order to stop Jeremiah has him arrested, beaten, and placed in stocks at the gate of the temple. [Stocks especially during the colonial period of history in this country served two purposes. The prisoner was put on public display as a warning to others and to open the prisoner up to mockery thus adding to the punishment.]

v.3 When released from his imprisonment, Jeremiah tells Pashhur that God has changed his name to Magor-Missabib which means "terror on every side" or "afraid of everything". We might say he will be called fraidy cat. In this case for good reason.

v.4 Pashhur will see the terror of friends and family, whom he has led to believe that there was nothing to fear, killed in battle or taken into captivity.

v.5 He will see the treasures of Jerusalem taken as spoil.

v.6 As for Pashhur, he and all his family will be taken to Babylon where they will die. Pashhur has brought much of this on himself by prophesying lies.

vv.7,8 At this point Jeremiah accuses God of tricking him into taking a job which has brought nothing but ridicule and hardship and threats.

v.9 Jeremiah says that he tried to spare himself by quitting his ministry. He said that he had decided not to speak God's message anymore. But he found that he couldn't quit. God's message was demanding to be let out. He had to preach it! [This is much the same statement made by Peter and John before the Jewish council in **Acts 4:19,20**.]

v.10 All Jeremiah's friends denounce him. They ridicule him, And they watch him like a hawk in order to catch him in some error so they can take their vengeance on him.

vv.11,12 God is still Jeremiah's protector. He will keep Jeremiah's enemies from succeeding in their plans. Jeremiah is ready to see God's action.

v.13 God is the defender of the poor and worthy of praise.

vv.14-18 In these verses we see Jeremiah at his lowest point thus far. His cry is, "I wish that I had never been born. If I were never born I would not be in this position." He calls for God to curse the man who announced his birth for not killing him in infancy. His reasoning is, "if I had died before birth my days would not be filled with shame and derision." He seems to be asking, "Was I just born to die in shame?"

These verses demonstrate that even the greatest servants of God still have periods of despair.

Chapter 21

v.1 Zedekiah sends counselors to Jeremiah to request that he petition the Lord on their behalf. [This takes place during the final siege of Jerusalem at about 588.]

v.2 Apparently Zedekiah is hoping for a miraculous deliverance from Nebuchadnezzar's army like Hezekiah had received when the Assyrians were threatening the city.

vv.3-10 *God's Answer to this Request - NO!*

vv.3,4 God says, "I will turn your own weapons against you" (remember the Midianites on the night Gideon and his 300 attacked). Not only will God not turn this enemy away, he will allow them to gather inside the city.

v.5 God, himself will fight against Judah with fury, anger, and wrath

v.6 He promises a plague or pestilence on man and beast.

v.7 Any who manage to survive the famine, sword, and plague of the siege will be turned over to Nebuchadnezzar and he will show no mercy.

vv.8,9 God's message to this people is, "If you want to save your life, go out and surrender. If you stay in the city you will die."

v.10 The defeat is sure because God has turned his back on the city. He has given it to the king of Babylon who will burn it.

vv.11-14 *A Warning to the Royal House*

v.12 Bring back justice. Protect and deliver the downtrodden and oppressed.

v.13 God was against Judah for their selfish pride and thinking that they were invincible.

v.14 They will be punished according to their actions.

God brings his judgment against nations just as surely as he will judge individuals.

Chapter 22

The First Verses of this Chapter Seem to Continue the Message at the End of Chapter 21

vv.1,2 Jeremiah is sent to deliver God's message to the rulers of Judah.

v.3 As was the case in 21:12 the king is called upon to remember and deliver the poor and downtrodden. It was their responsibility to return justice to Judah.

v.4 The promise is if they will operate in a just manner then there will continue to be descendants of David on the throne and the kingdom will continue.

v.5 If they refuse the kingdom will come to an end.

v.6 God is saying even though they had been a luscious, beautiful, well watered country, he would turn them into wilderness.

v.7 Two suggested ideas here: Either God is saying he would devastate the nation like a forest fire or he is being more literal in saying that all the cedar used to build up the glorious city will be thrown into the fire. The picture is much the same.

v.8 When people from other nations view the destruction they will wonder why the Lord would destroy his great city.

v.9 The answer will be because they have broken covenant and worshipped other gods.

v.10 Don't weep for dead king Josiah. Weep for those who will be taken away and never see home again. [Jehoahaz or Shallum.]

vv.11-30 *is a Series of Messages Directed Toward the Sons of Josiah. Josiah's Reign Will be Followed by the Reigns of Three Sons and a Grandson (Jehoahaz, Jehoiakim, Jehoiachin, Zedekiah)*

vv.11,12 Shallum or Jehoahaz was taken captive by Pharaoh Necho of Egypt. He never returned, but died in Egypt.

vv.13-17 These woes are spoken against Jehoiakim for building on the backs of the poor. He withheld wages and used forced labor to build a bigger cedar palace. The message that is delivered is it takes more than a cedar palace to be a great king.

vv.15,16 Josiah, his father did justice as he judged the case of the poor and needy. This was doing God's will or knowing God. (See **Micah 6:8**)

v.17 Josiah's sons on the other hand only had eyes for their own wants and thus practiced oppression and violence.

vv.18,19 No one will cry at Jehoiakim's funeral. He will receive no regal burial instead he will be dragged out and dropped in a hole like a donkey. [His life ended in shame and disgrace.]

v.20 The nations they had trusted are no more. God is their only help.

v.21 When times were good God had given warnings but they would not listen.

v.22 Now all of their shepherds (leaders) will be swept away and even those in the palaces (cedars of Lebanon) will groan.

v.24 Jeconiah (Jehoiachin) will be cast off as king.

v.25 He will be given over to his enemies.

vv.26,27 He and his mother will be taken captive and die in a foreign land. He will not return.

vv.28-30 Because of his rebellion and wickedness Jehoiachin might as well have been childless (he had 7 sons) for he will have no descendants come to the throne.

NOTES

Chapter 23

Much of this Chapter Deals with God's Anger Toward Israel's False Leaders

vv.1,2 Woe to the shepherds of Israel who destroy the sheep. The reason Judah was in the shape they were in could be traced to the prophets, priests, and kings who led them in idolatry. Where it is the shepherds job to lead and protect the sheep in his care, these men were scattering and destroying God's sheep. Here God says that they will be replaced.

vv.3,4 In these verses there is the hope of restoration. The scattered sheep will be gathered and brought home and faithful shepherds will be placed over them.

vv.5,6 These verses definitely speak of the coming Messiah. He will be of the branch of David, he will bring salvation to Israel, and his name will be "The Lord is Righteous."

vv.7,8 Since the parents had failed to teach their children to keep the covenant God made with them after leaving Egypt, the children did not know God. God will be remembered more for his deliverance from Babylonian captivity.

v.9 Jeremiah is incapacitated by the conflict between the false message of the prophets and God's true message.

v.10 The land is cursed because these false shepherds have led the people away from God in rebellion.

vv.11,12 Prophet and priest are ungodly. They have even brought their idolatrous practices into the temple itself. So, God will bring them down.

vv.13,14 Where the prophets of the Northern kingdom had been bad in their practice of Baal worship and prophesying by Baal, the priests and prophets in the South had been worse. They had been practicing adultery and lies, and were so bad that God says Jerusalem was now like Sodom and Gomorrah.

v.15 As the result of their wickedness they will taste the bitterness of the wrath of God.

v.16 DON'T LISTEN TO THESE FALSE PROPHETS! Their message is from their own imagination and not from God.

v.17 Their lying message gave false hope.

vv.18-22 These false prophets are not privy to the council of God. Their message is not God's message. So, they are bringing the storm of God's wrath. God's anger will continue until his plan is accomplished. These prophets were not sent by God. If they had known God's mind and God's will they would have called men to repentance.

vv.23,24 God is near. God is far. God is everywhere. (**Psalm 139:7-10**)

vv.25-28 These false prophets place great stock in dreams, but their message is filled with lies and deceit and causes men to forget God. God said if you have a dream, tell it and if you have a message from God tell it. The difference will be as great as the difference between straw and grain.

v.29 God's word is nourishing and it is powerful. [The Hebrews writer delivered the same message in **Heb 4:12**]

vv.30-32 God is against these prophets who get their message from one another and not from him. They lie in saying their message is from him. They lead the people astray by dreams and lies. God says he did not send them. As such they do not profit the people {they do them no good}.

vv.33-40 Apparently these false prophets were drawing attention to their message by claiming it was an oracle from God. God said do not use that phrase. You may ask what the Lord has spoken or what the Lord has answered but do not run around claiming the burden of the Lord. These false teachers were perverting God's message. God says they will be cast away and will suffer everlasting reproach.

NOTES

Chapter 24

This Chapter Contains God's Message to Judah of a day of Division and Judgment. God Delivers this Message Through a Vision of Two Baskets of Figs.

Verses 1-3 *Contain the Vision Itself then God's Explanation is Given in the Remainder of the Chapter*

v.1 This vision came at the beginning of Zedekiah's reign. God showed Jeremiah two baskets of figs which had been brought to the temple. [I see in this a demonstration of the kinds of givers that dwelled in Jerusalem: those who give their best and those felt that they had to give something but did not want to give up the best that they had. (See **Malachi 1:6-8; 3:8-10**) The gift is a demonstration of what is in the heart. {Cain and Abel.}]

vv.2,3 One of the two baskets Jeremiah saw contained very good figs while the other basket contained figs that were inedible.

Verses 4-7 *Contain God's Message Concerning the "Good Figs"*

vv.4,5 The good figs represent the best of Judah which had already been taken captive to Babylon. In that group God saw the good, worthwhile and fruitful from the people.

v.6 God says he has set his eyes for good toward them. They will be blessed instead of cursed; planted and built up instead of being torn down and destroyed.

v.7 These individuals have a penitent, teachable heart. They have a desire to know and please God. There is hope for these people. They can be brought back to God.

Verses 8-10 *Show the Contrasting Group Which God Says are the "Bad Figs"*

v.8 Zedekiah and the rabble which have been left, even those who have escaped to Egypt are the bad figs. These have no desire to please God. They care nothing for God.

v.9 They will be delivered to trouble. They will find trouble wherever they go. They refuse to submit to God so God has given them up and is not their protector anymore.

v.10 They will be consumed.

Chapter 25

vv1,2 This particular message came in the fourth year of Jehoiakim which was the first year of Nebuchadnezzar (actually would be co-regent with his father two more years). This was the year that Babylon defeated Pharaoh Necho at Charchemesh. Jeremiah delivered this message to all of Jerusalem and Judah.

v.3 Jeremiah says he had been prophesying for 23 years yet the people had not listened to him.

v.4 God had continually sent prophets but they did not listen.

vv.5,6 All of these prophets had delivered the message that if Judah wanted to continue to go on and be blessed by God they would have to repent. They must not go after idols or provoke God to anger. If they heeded this warning they would be allowed to stay in the land unharmed by God.

v.7 Jeremiah's message at this time was, "You did not listen and have provoked God to your own hurt."

vv.8,9 You will fall when God brings the armies of Babylon to conquer and devastate the nations which surround Judah.

v.10 When this happens your joyful occasions will be gone (bride and bride groom), everyday work will cease (mill grinding), all signs of life will be gone (lighting of candles).

v.11 The land will be completely devastated 70 years while Judah served Babylon.

vv.12-14 {God's judgment against Babylon.} They will be punished for their wickedness at the end of this 70 year period. The surrounding nations would devastate them. They will be repaid for their iniquity.

The Remainder of this Chapter Describes the Process of God's Wrath Against those Nations that had Done Evil and Provoked Him

vv.15-17 Jeremiah is to take this message of God's fury to the nations. [Several of the O.T. prophets brought a message of God's wrath against nations other than Israel or Judah.]

v.18 Jerusalem and Judah will be turned to devastation (a place of astonishment, hissing, and curse). This has already begun.

v.19 Egypt will also feel the wrath of the sword of God.

vv.20-26 The mixed Arab lands will not be spared. Looking at this list this included all of the nations surrounding Palestine. Some of them are called by the name of one of the descendants of Abraham through Keturah's children or through Ishmael, Babylon will be last in the list (Sheshach).

vv.27-33 All the nations will be made to drink the cup of God's wrath. If he did not spare his own people (Jerusalem), how will the heathen nations escape? God will bring his wrath against the wicked.

vv.34-38 The Leaders (shepherds) should wail because they have lost their sheep. They failed to lead and protect and the Lord will come like a lion out of his lair and leave them desolate.

Chapter 26

vv.1,2 God sends Jeremiah to the Temple to prophecy. He was to deliver the message full force in this place where worship had been profaned.

v.3 The hope was that the people would repent and God could relent of the calamity he had planned for rebellious Judah.

vv.4-6 God's warning is that if they will not listen and repent Jerusalem will be made like Shiloh (**Jer. 7:12**). {Shiloh was the location of the ark and the center of worship from the days of Joshua through Samuel. After the loss of the ark of the covenant to the Philistines, Shiloh was never a place of great importance again. It is thought that maybe the Tabernacle was destroyed during the Philistine invasion. Shiloh was in the region of Ephraim which became the leading tribe of the Northern kingdom.}

vv.7-9 This message from Jeremiah caused a mob scene. The prophets, priests, and people seized Jeremiah and sought to kill him. They did not want his message.

vv.10-16 *The Trial of Jeremiah*

v.10 The princes (city officials) came to the gate of the Temple to judge Jeremiah.

v.11 The charges - Jeremiah speaks against this city and deserves to die.

vv.12-15 Jeremiah's defense - "God sent me with this message. It is a message of hope. If you will amend your ways and repent, God will relent. I am in your hands. If you kill me you will be guilty of innocent blood."

v.16 The verdict - This man does not deserve to die. He was delivering God's message.

vv.17-19 Here we have a reminder that Micah had delivered a similar message in the days of Hezekiah and was not executed for his message. Instead the people repented and the city was spared.

vv.20-23 *The Case of Uriah*

v.20 Uriah delivered a message like Jeremiah's.

v.21 King Jehoiakim sought to kill him. Uriah ran to Egypt in fear.

v.22 Elnathan was sent to bring Uriah back from Egypt.

v.23 Uriah was brought back to Jehoiakim and executed.

v.24 Jeremiah was saved from a similar fate by Ahikam.

Chapter 27

This Chapter can be Broken into Three Sections: 1) God's Message to the Surrounding Nations 2) God's Message to Zedekiah 3) God's Message to the Priests

vv.1,2 [In the beginning of the reign of Jehoiakim or Zedekiah. There is a discrepancy in the manuscripts at this point some say one, some the other. From the rest of the chapter it seems that this probably took place in about the third year of Zedekiah. Whichever king was in place, God's message would be the same.] Jeremiah is told by God to make a yoke and wear it as an illustration of the message he was delivering from God. He may have made as many as seven yokes (one for himself and one for each of the recipients of the message).

v.3 Jeremiah was to send this message to the kings of Moab, Ammon, Tyre, and Sidon by means of the king's emissaries.

vv.4,5 This message is from God, the creator, who can do as he wishes with men, animals, nations, and lands for he made them.

vv.6,7 All of these nations will be given into the control of Babylon during the days of Nebuchadnezzar, his son, and his grandson, until the time comes that Babylon, itself, is overthrown. These nations will be placed under the yoke of Babylon.

v.8 Any nation that will not submit to Babylon will be overthrown and destroyed.

vv.9,10 All prophets who say otherwise are lying and will cause those who listen to them to be driven from their land and destroyed.

v.11 Those who submit to the yoke of Babylon will be allowed to remain in their land.

vv.12,13 To Zedekiah - Why will you die? Submit to Babylon and live. Why bring sword, famine and pestilence needlessly?

vv.14,15 The prophets who tell you that you will not serve Babylon are lying. They are not from God and will cause you to be driven out and killed.

v.16 To the priests - "Don't listen to the prophets who say the treasures of the temple will be returned soon. They lie."

v.17 Serve the king of Babylon and live.

v.18 If these were true prophets they would be praying that the rest of the treasures of Jerusalem not be taken as well.

vv.19-22 The truth is all the brass from the temple and the rest of the treasures that had been left will also be taken to Babylon where they will stay until God brings them back. [This will not happen until the reign of Cyrus of Persia.]

Chapter 28

This Chapter Contains One of the Narrative Sections of the Book of Jeremiah. The Events Take Place at About the Same Time as the Events of Chapter 27 as We See a Continuation of the Yoke Lesson. At this Time Jeremiah is Still Wearing a Wooden Yoke as an Illustration of Babylonian Bondage.

v.1 In the fifth month of the year Hananiah, the son of Azur from Gibeon (a city north of Jerusalem about 10 miles), confronts Jeremiah in the temple and contradicts his prophecy.

v.2 His message is "God says Babylon's yoke is broken!"

v.3 Hananiah sets a time table for the restoration of all that has been taken by Babylon. "Within 2 years all the temple treasures will be returned."

v.4 At the same time all the captives (including Jehoiachin) will come home.

vv.5-9 *Contains Jeremiah's Response to this Prophecy*

v.6 Amen (may it be so) may God perform your words. May all that has been taken be returned. Jeremiah truly would have loved for Hananiah to be right but he knew better.

vv.7-9 These verses contain a reminder of the test of a true prophet. (See **Deut. 18:20-22**) You could recognize a true prophet if what he prophesied came about. If it did not happen as he said he was a false prophet and worthy of death.

vv.10,11 At this point Hananiah dramatically took the yoke from Jeremiah's neck and broke it saying this is the way God has broken the yoke of Babylon. Jeremiah went his way.

v.12 God gave Jeremiah a message for Hananiah.

vv.13,14 You broke a yoke of wood. It will be replaced by a yoke of iron (more severe). Nebuchadnezzar will rule over the nations and even over the wild beasts.

v.15 God has not sent you. You have caused this people to believe a lie.

v.16 You will die as the result of your rebellion and leading Judah in rebellion.

v.17 Two months later Hananiah died.

Chapter 29

vv.1-3 God has Jeremiah send a letter to the captives in Babylon (elders, royalty, priests, prophets, all the people). This letter was sent after Jeconiah (Jehoiachin) had been taken captive and was carried to Babylon by Elasah and Gemariah, envoys sent by King Zedekiah.

vv.4-7 The message was, "settle in. Build houses, plant gardens, marry, choose mates for your children. Work for the good of the land where you are captive for it will be better for you if the land prospers." In other words he was telling them to act like they were going to be there for a long while.

vv.8,9 Don't trust the diviners and prophets who tell you that you will only have a short stay in Babylon. They lie. God did not send them.

vv.10-14 A message of hope - After the 70 years are completed God promises to visit the captives and return them home. God says, "I desire peace and not evil." His message is, "Seek me, pray to me, search for me with all of your heart and you will find me. I will bring you back from captivity."

vv.15-20 It is a blessing to have prophets from God only when they are heeded - God tells these captives that those who remain in Judah are facing sword, famine, and pestilence because they have failed to heed the message of the prophets whom God had sent time and again.

vv.21-23 God's judgment against Zedekiah and Ahab - They will be turned over to Nebuchadnezzar for punishment. They are false prophets and adulterers. Their punishment will be so severe that from that time on if you wanted to curse someone all you would have to say is, "God make you like Zedekiah and Ahab whom Nebuchadnezzar roasted."

vv.24-32 The case against Shemaiah the Nehelamite - Shemaiah wrote letters back to Judah especially to Zephaniah, the priest. He told him, "It is your responsibility to put in prison and the stocks every demented man and false prophet. Why then, haven't you punished Jeremiah. Jeremiah has told us to settle in to Babylon as if we would be here a long time." Zephaniah read this letter to Jeremiah and Jeremiah sent God's message back. The message was, "God says I have not sent Shemaiah. He does not speak for me. He has caused you to trust a lie. He and his family will be punished. They will not see the good that I bring because he has preached rebellion."

Chapter 30

This Chapter and the Next One Provide a Hope of Restoration

vv.1-3 God tells Jeremiah to write all of the message God has given him down in a book or on a scroll. This way there will be a record of God's promise of restoration following the period of punishment.

vv.4-7 Now is a time of panic and pain. Men groan and are in pain equal to a woman in labor. There is nothing equal to this time of trouble, but Israel shall be saved out of it.

vv.8,9 The yoke of the oppressor will be broken. There will be no more slavery to foreigners. Instead they will serve the Lord and be ruled by a descendant of David whom he will raise up (messianic prophesy).

v.10 God will save you from afar and bring you back from captivity.

v.11 Even though God is going to bring a full end to the oppressing nations, Israel will not be completely destroyed. They will be chastised and punished for their iniquity.

vv.12,13 God says, "Right now you are in a deplorable condition. You have apparently incurable wounds and afflictions, you have no one to plead your case, and there is no relief in sight.

v.14 You are deserted by your lovers (allies), and God has punished you grievously because of your sins.

v.15 You have nothing to cry about because you brought this on yourself.

v.16 Your oppressors will be oppressed.

v.17 At the same time God will heal your wounds.

vv.18-22 *The Promise of Restoration*
The cities will be rebuilt. The palace will be restored. Thanksgiving will be renewed in the land. God will once again be Israel's protector to punish the oppressors. The nobles and governors will draw near to God. They will pledge themselves to seek God and once again will be seen by God to be his people.

vv.23,24 God's fury will go forth like whirlwind on the wicked. It will not stop until it has achieved God's purpose. All of this will be easier to understand in the future.

Chapter 31

Chapter 30 Ends with God's Wrath Running Its Course

v.1 At that time Israel will be mine again.

v.2 As the survivors of the wilderness wanderings found favor with God, so also will the remnant of Israel.

v.3 God's love is everlasting. He will draw Israel back by his love.

v.4 Israel will be rebuilt. Times of rejoicing and reasons for joy will return.

v.5 As an example the vines would be replanted and enjoyed. The vine and its fruit are often pictures of rejoicing.

v.6 The picture of a return to Zion for worship is a picture of Israel and Judah reuniting in worship to God. Israel had not worshipped in Jerusalem since the days of Jeroboam.

vv.7-9 The Lord will save the remnant of Israel. Rejoice. All will come home both weak and strong. God says I will provide and protect.

vv.10-14 All nations can rejoice. God is redeeming Jacob. The times of sorrow will be passed as God prospers them once more. Their sorrow will be turned to joy.

vv.15-22 God's mercy is proclaimed toward Ephraim (Israel). Though there had been cause for mourning, that time is past. They now have hope. Because of God's chastisement Israel has now turned back to God. {Matthew quotes v.15 in **Matt. 2:17-18**. Severe mourning took place in the region of Bethlehem when Herod slaughtered the boys 2 years old and younger in an effort to kill the Christ. Matthew says this is a fulfillment of Jeremiah's prophecy.} O.T. prophecies often had both near and far meaning.

v.20 Even though Israel had been rebellious, God still loved them.

vv.21,22 Follow the markers and come back home. Things will be as different as a woman protecting a man. {This may also have reference to the virgin birth.}

v.23 Judah will also be returned from captivity.

v.24 Life will be returned to normal.

v.25 The hungry will be filled and the sorrowful will be comforted.

v.26 Sweet sleep is one more reference to joy being restored.

vv.27,28 What had been torn down and driven out will be restored.

vv.29,30 Children will not pay the penalty of their parents sin, each will answer for himself.

vv.31-34 Here we have the promise of the new covenant. This passage is repeated in **Hebrews 8**. Under the Old covenant Jews were born physically a part of the covenant. For this reason as they grew they had to be taught to know, love, and serve God. Under the New covenant believers, those who know God and choose to serve him, are born spiritually into the covenant at baptism.

vv.35-37 When the laws of nature change and the universe can be completely measured, God will cease loving. This is another way of saying God's love never ceases.

vv.38-41 Jerusalem will be rebuilt.

Chapter 32

vv.1-5 *Jeremiah Imprisoned in the Palace*

v.1 These events took place during the 10th year of Zedekiah's reign and the 18th year of Nebuchadnezzar.

v.2 Jerusalem is under siege from Babylon and Jeremiah is imprisoned.

vv.3-5 Zedekiah has Jeremiah imprisoned because he has said that Jerusalem will fall to the Babylonians, that Zedekiah will be captured and taken to Babylon, and that they would not succeed against Babylon (prophesies that were being fulfilled at that time).

vv.6-15 *The Land Purchase*

vv.6,7 God tells Jeremiah that his uncle, Hanameel, is going to ask him to buy a piece of property.

v.8 Hanameel does what God said that he would.

vv.9-12 Jeremiah buys the property and has the deed signed sealed and witnessed.

vv.13-15 Baruch is told to put the deed up in a safe place for houses and lands will one day be purchased again.

vv.16-25 *Jeremiah Prays for an Explanation*

vv.16-22 Jeremiah speaks first of God's power, lovingkindness, and faithfulness seen in the deliverance from Egypt and his bringing Israel to the promised land.

vv.23,24 He then speaks of Israel's disobedience and God's punishment. As a result the city is under siege.

v.25 Why buy land when the city is given to the Chaldeans?

vv.26-44 *God's Answer*

vv.26,27 As God I can do anything I choose. Nothing is too hard for me.

vv.28,29 The city will be given to the Babylonians who will burn it including all the houses where Baal was worshipped.

vv.30-35 Here we have a reminder of the rebellion and rejection of God which had been practiced by Israel. God has constantly been provoked to anger. This people have refused to listen to his warnings. They defiled the temple. They burn their children as offerings to Molech. This disgusts God.

vv.36-44 [Hope section.] I will bring them back. They will once again be my people and I will be their God. God will give them a heart for him. God will renew the covenant. Just as he has driven them from their homes and lands, he will bring them back and they will buy lands again. They can even buy lands now because the captives will return.

Chapter 33

v.1 This prophecy occurs while Jeremiah is imprisoned.

vv.2,3 God, the all-powerful creator is in control and will give answer to those who seek him.

vv.4,5 The situation at this time in Jerusalem was deplorable. Houses have been torn down to repair breeches in the walls. The empty places where those houses stood are now depositories for dead bodies. God has hidden his face from Israel because of their wickedness. (See **Isaiah 59:1,2**)

vv.6-13 *THE PROMISE OF RESTORATION (This Section Pictures a Complete Reversal of the Present Conditions.)*

v.6 Health, healing, peace, and truth will return to the land.

v.7 The captives will come home.

v.8 God will forgive and cleanse his people. [This is a picture of justification.]

v.9 Jerusalem will then have the name of joy and praise rather than being a place of hissing and cursing.

vv.10-13 The desolate ruins will become a place of rejoicing. Shepherds will once again bring their flocks. The city will be a place of praise to God.

vv.14-18 *THE PROMISED MESSIAH*

v.14 The days are coming when God's promise to Israel and Judah will be fulfilled.

v.15 A branch of righteousness from the lineage of David will rule.

v.16 Salvation, safety, and righteousness will come.

v.17 This is a reminder of God's promise to David. God is here saying that he remembers and will keep his promises.

v.18 The regular worship of the people to God will also be restored. [Books of **Ezra** and **Nehemiah**.]

vv.19-26 *THE ASSURANCE OF THE PROMISE*

vv.19-21 If God's covenant with creation can be broken then his lesser covenants and promises will be broken as well. {When the sun ceases to rise and the seasons fail to come in order every year then you can worry about God not keeping his promises.}

v.22 God's people will once again be numberless. [Promise to Abraham **Gen.15:5**]

vv.23,24 Here we see a bit of the mockery from the nations. "It is too bad God has cast away Israel and Judah so they cease to be a nation." [Note: This might be a lament that due to the captivity and destruction Jerusalem was suffering, God's promises to David and Levi cannot be fulfilled. I lean toward this view.]

vv.25,26 God reminds once again, "When I no longer keep my promises to creation, when the sun ceases to rise then I will no longer have mercy on my people. The captives will come home.

Chapter 34

v.1 The siege is dying down and Jerusalem is about to fall. These are the final days of Zedekiah.

v.2 Jeremiah is sent by God to tell Zedekiah that Jerusalem will fall to Babylon and be burned.

v.3 Zedekiah will not be able to escape from the Babylonian force at the fall of the kingdom. [Note: He did attempt to escape when the end became eminent.] Jeremiah tells Zedekiah that he will actually see Nebuchadnezzar and speak with him face to face then be taken to Babylon.

vv.4,5 God promises Zedekiah that he will not fall by the sword but instead will die in peace in Babylon. He will have full funeral rites performed.

vv.6,7 All of this was spoken when Nebuchadnezzar was finishing off the last of the fortified cities of Judah.

The Covenant to Release the Hebrew Slaves

vv.8,9 A covenant (binding agreement) was made at this time to set at liberty all Hebrew slaves being held in Judah at this time. It was not right to hold brethren as slaves.

v.10 At first everyone went along with this agreement and kept this covenant.

v.11 For some reason the people rejected this covenant and took back their word and their slaves.

v.12 God has a message for these treacherous individuals.

vv.13,14 This is a reminder of the Jubilee law in which all Hebrew slaves were released back to their families if they so desired. Every 7 years the slaves were to be set free. This law had not been kept.

v.15 God says, "You finally did the right thing by freeing your brethren."

v.16 "Then you turned around and made them slaves once again."

v.17 God then says, "Since you failed to obey and free your brethren from slavery I will free you from your lives." [In breaking this vow they literally profaned the name of God. They broke their promise to God.]

vv.18,19 God says, "I will make these covenant breakers like the calf they split when they made this covenant promise." [The splitting of the sacrifice animal and walking between the parts signified the sentiment that they were worthy of death if they broke that promise.] God is telling them they would indeed die a terrible death. {Abraham's covenant with God in **Gen. 15:10ff**}

v.20 The bodies of these covenant breakers will be left carrion for the birds.

v.21 Zedekiah and his princes will be given over to the enemy.

v.22 Even though Nebuchadnezzar had let up on the siege so he might focus attention on war with Egypt, he will be called back by God to finish destroying the city of Jerusalem.

Chapter 35

v.1 This event takes place during the days of Jehoiakim's reign. [This means that they take place at an earlier time than the events recorded in the past few chapters.]

v.2 God tells Jeremiah to bring the family of Rechab into one of the chambers of the temple and give them wine. {The Rechabites were Kenites, a tribe of Midian, and may have been descended from Moses' father-in-law Jethro. Jehonadab, the founder of this group helped Jehu overthrow the family of Ahab. The worship of Baal was offensive to them. Jehonadab placed strict restrictions on his family to avoid town life.[1]

vv.3-5 Jeremiah brings what appears to be all the men of Rechab's family into one of the chambers of the temple, sets wine before them and tells them to drink.

v.6 They refuse the wine based upon their commitment to Jonadab not to drink wine as he had commanded them.

v.7 Jonadab had also told them not to build houses or plant crops or vineyards but to live in tents as Nomads.

vv.8-10 These people have obeyed all of these commands. They live in tents, do not plant, and do not drink wine.

v.11 The reason they are living in Jerusalem at this time is for safety from the invading Babylonian and Syrian armies.

---

[1] F.N. Peloubet, "Rechab", *Peloubet's Bible Dictionary* (Philadelphia: Universal Book and Bible House, 1925), p. 550.

vv.12-15 God's message to the men of Judah - Look at the Rechabites. Their patriarch told them not to drink wine and they obey to this day (approx. 250 years[2]). I ,God, have spoken to you and you do not obey. I even sent prophets to call you back and you still don't obey.

v.16 To summarize - The Rechabites still obey their father but you won't obey me.

v.17 Because of disobedience all the promised calamity will come against Jerusalem and Judah.

vv.18,19 To the Rechabites - Because of your obedience and faithfulness your family will not be wiped out.

---

[2] ibid.

Chapter 36

vv.1,2 In approximately 605 B.C. (fourth year of Jehoiakim) God tells Jeremiah to write down all of his prophecies in a book or on a scroll. [This would have been about 20 years of material and thus would be a clear sign of inspiration.]

v.3 The purpose of recording this material is to bring rebellious Judah to repentance and back to God.

v.4 Jeremiah dictated all of the message to Baruch who then wrote it down on the scroll. [This is the same Baruch who took care of the land transfer for Jeremiah.]

vv.5-7 For some reason Jeremiah was restricted from the temple at this time so he instructs Baruch to go to the temple at the next fast and read the scroll to all the people of Judah who came to the fast. Again the hope is to bring Judah to repentance. Jeremiah was hoping a knowledge of God's anger would bring this result.

v.8 Baruch carries out these orders.

vv.9,10 In the 5th year of Jehoiakim in the 9th month (this would be around December and about 1 year after God's command to write down the prophecy) a day of fasting was declared and Baruch went to the temple and read the scroll from the upper court near Gemariah's room.

vv.11-13 Michaiah, the son of Gemariah, heard Baruch read the scroll then went to tell the king's officials what he had heard.

vv.14,15 These officials summoned Baruch and had him read the scroll to them.

v.16 The message struck fear in their hearts and they decided that the king needed to hear it also.

vv.17,18 First they asked Baruch how he got this message and he told them that Jeremiah had dictated it to him.

v.19 These officials warned Jeremiah and Baruch to hide while they brought the matter to the king's attention.

v.20 The king is told of the scroll.

v.21 Jehoiakim sends Jehudi for the scroll and has him read it.

v.22 Jehoiakim is in his winter house and near the fire.

v.23 Jehoiakim cuts out and burns each section of the scroll as it is being read. [It seems he believes that if the scroll no longer exists, the message of the scroll will cease to exist as well.]

v.24 He was not afraid or moved to repentance.

v.25 His officials begged him not to burn the scroll but he would not listen to them.

v.26 Jehoiakim next tried to arrest Jeremiah and Baruch but was unsuccessful because God had hidden them.

vv.27,28 God then tells Jeremiah to re-write the scroll. [Kings cannot stop the purposes of God.]

vv.29-31 God has Jeremiah tell Jehoiakim that even though he does not want to believe that the King of Babylon will overrun and destroy Jerusalem and all in it, IT WILL HAPPEN. Jehoiakim and his family will be casualties of war. (Note: Even though Jehoiakim's son, Jehoiachin, did come to the throne it was only for about a month.)

v.32 Jeremiah and Baruch rewrote the scroll with added words.

Chapter 37

v.1 Nebuchadnezzar had removed Jehoiachin and made his uncle Zedekiah king instead.

v.2 Zedekiah did not pay attention to the word of God any better than his predecessors had.

v.3 Zedekiah did send to Jeremiah with a request for prayers.

v.4 At this time Jeremiah. was still free to come and go as he wished.

v.5 Pharaoh's army has come to relieve Jerusalem and the army of Babylon has lifted the siege to go meet them in battle.

vv.6-10 God's message to Zedekiah is the Egyptians will go back home and when they do the Babylonians will return to finish taking the city and burning it. Even if all that was left of the Babylonian army were the weak and wounded they would still be able to burn Jerusalem.

vv.11,12 While the siege was lifted Jeremiah tried to go home to Anathoth to take care of some personal business.

v.13 At the Benjamin Gate he was arrested by Irijah for defection to the Chaldeans.

vv.14-16 Jeremiah claimed innocence in this matter but was still taken to the officials who hated him and was beaten and cast into a dungeon cell.

v.17 Zedekiah sent for Jeremiah secretly and asked for the Lord's message. The message was that he would be given over to the king of Babylon. At this point Jeremiah asks some questions and makes a request of Zedekiah.

v.18 "What crime have I committed?"

v.19 "Why aren't the false prophets imprisoned?"

vv.20,21 Jeremiah then begged not to be taken back to the dungeon lest he die there. Zedekiah showed kindness and mercy by jailing him in the palace and seeing to it that he received daily bread for as long as there was bread in the city.

Chapter 38

The Material in this Chapter is a Continuation of the Narrative in Chapter 37

v.1 The men listed here are a group of advisors/government officials that are opposed to Jeremiah and his message that have heard Jeremiah's advice to the remaining inhabitants of Jerusalem.

vv.2,3 Jeremiah's message to the people was to surrender to the Babylonians so that they could save their lives. By this point the city is all but defeated.

v.4 The group of officials told Zedekiah that Jeremiah deserved to die for destroying the morale of the remaining soldiers with his "treasonous speech". They accused him of weakening the hands of the defenders of the city.

v.5 Zedekiah's weak response was, "I can't stop you."

v.6 The dungeon Jeremiah was cast into was actually a dry cistern. The water was gone and only mud remained.

vv.7-13 *EBED-MELECH'S RESCUE MISSION*

v.7 Ebed-Melech, an Ethiopian (Cushite) eunuch advisor to Zedekiah, learned of Jeremiah's harsh treatment.

vv.8,9 He then went to Zedekiah to report on the severity of Jeremiah's condition. He feared that if Jeremiah were left where he was he would die of either starvation, exposure, or both.

v.10 Zedekiah decisively commanded that Ebed-Melech take 30 men and rescue Jeremiah.

vv.11-13 In an act of second-mile kindness Ebed-Melech took rags to cushion the ropes so that Jeremiah would not be injured as he was pulled from the pit. Following this rescue Jeremiah remained a prisoner in the palace court.

ZEDEKIAH SEEKS ADVICE FROM JEREMIAH AGAIN

v.14 Zedekiah has Jeremiah brought to him where he questions him secretly.

v.15 Jeremiah's initial response was, "If I told you what you want to know, you would not listen to me and might have me killed."

v.16 Zedekiah swears not to kill Jeremiah.

vv.17,18 The advice is simple: "If you will surrender to the Babylonians you will save the lives of you and your family and this city will not be burned. If you refuse the city will be burned and you will not escape."

v.19 Zedekiah claims that he is afraid he will be turned over to the Jews that have already defected to the Babylonians and they will torture him.

v.20 Jeremiah assures Zedekiah that this will not happen and pleads with him to surrender so that it will be well with him.

vv.21-23 Jeremiah goes on to say that if Zedekiah does not surrender, the women that are left in the palace will be given to the Chaldeans and will say to Zedekiah, "Your friends gave you bad advice. They led you wrong and then turned their backs on you." Jeremiah then emphasized that Zedekiah would not escape and the city would be burned.

vv.24-26 Zedekiah, desiring to keep their conversation secret, told Jeremiah that if he were to be asked what they talked about he was to say that he had been pleading not to be taken back to the prison in the house of Jonathan where he would die.

vv.27,28 When the princes asked about the conversation Jeremiah followed Zedekiah's wishes. Jeremiah will remain imprisoned until the fall of Jerusalem.

NOTES

Chapter 39

v.1 In the 9th year and 10th month of Zedekiah's reign Nebuchadnezzar began his final siege of Jerusalem.

v.2 In the 11th year and 4th month (approximately one and one half years later) the city was breached and the walls penetrated.

v.3 The Babylonian officials set up in the middle gate of the city, a place where business would be transacted, to demonstrate that they are now in charge.

v.4 Zedekiah and his officials try to sneak out of the city after dark and run for their lives. [Jeremiah had urged Zedekiah to surrender to save his life and the city. Now it is too late.]

v.5 Zedekiah is captured near Jericho. He is then taken north to Riblah in Syria to be tried before Nebuchadnezzar.

vv.6,7 Zedekiah is forced to watch the execution of his sons and nobles before having his eyes put out, being chained and taken to Babylon.

v.8 As Jeremiah had prophesied the city is then burned and the walls torn down.

v.9 The remnant of the people and those who had defected are taken to Babylon as captives.

v.10 Some of the poorest are left behind and given lands and vineyards.

vv.11,12 Nebuchadnezzar leaves orders to free Jeremiah and give him whatever he wants.

vv.13,14 Jeremiah is freed from the court of the prison and committed to the care of Gedaliah.

vv.15-18 During the final days of Jerusalem Jeremiah received instructions from God concerning Ebed-Melech, the Egyptian. God tells Ebed-Melech that he is bringing his judgment on Jerusalem but Ebed-Melech will be spared, protected and freed because he had put his trust in the Lord.

{The events of the fall of Jerusalem are also recorded in **2 Kings 25** and **2 Chronicles 36**.)

Chapter 40

v.1 Jeremiah is being led in chains toward Babylon with the rest of the exiles following the fall of Jerusalem until they reach Ramah, the departure point.

vv.2,3 At Ramah Nebuzaradan, the captain charged with rescuing Jeremiah, removes Jeremiah's chains and explains that the present destruction of Jerusalem is what had been promised by God as a punishment for Judah's sin and rebellion. [Here we see God delivering his message through a pagan general.]

vv.4,5 Jeremiah is then given his choice of where to go. He can go to Babylon where Nebuzaradan promises he will care for him, or he can go back to Judah and live under the oversight of Gedaliah, the man made governor of the region by the Babylonians. In short, he has been set free to go wherever he wants to.

v.6 Jeremiah decides to go back to Mizpah and live with the remnant left behind by the Babylonians under the oversight and care of Gedaliah.

vv.7,8 Several military commanders that had not been captured by the Babylonians come back in with their men when they hear that Gedaliah is the Babylonian appointed governor.

vv.9,10 Gedaliah tells them not to be afraid to live in the land and serve the Chaldeans. He will serve as the spokesman to give the regular reports to Babylon and they can go home to their cities, gather their crops and live a normal life.

vv.11,12 Refugees that had fled to Ammon, Moab, Edom, and other outlying areas come back to Judah as well when word gets out of

Gedaliah's governorship. They also help to harvest the bumper crop of produce of that year.

Warning to Gedaliah

vv.13,14 The returning army officers warn Governor Gedaliah of a plot to assassinate him planned by Baalis, king of the Ammonites. Gedaliah does not believe their report.

v.15 Johanan even comes to Gedaliah secretly and offers to kill Ishmael, the named assassin before he can carry out his plan. The fear is if Gedaliah is killed then the weak remnant that has been left behind by the Babylonians will be scattered and perish.

v.16 Gedaliah refuses to allow Johanan to kill Ishmael because he does not believe that the plot is true.

Chapter 41

Bear in Mind that Originally the Bible was not Divided into Chapters and Verses. This Being True Often Times Chapter Breaks Occur in the Middle of a Narrative or Thought. The Events of Chapter 41 Should be Taken to be a Continuation of the Events at the End of Chapter 40.

v.1 Ishmael, whom Gedaliah trusted, came with 10 men and was welcomed by Gedaliah. [The text points out that Ishmael was of royal birth and had been an officer of the king.]

vv.2,3 During the meal Ishmael and his men assassinate Gedaliah and all the Jews and Babylonians that were with him in the house. [This is what Johanan had warned Gedaliah would happen at the end of chapter 40.]

vv.4-8 The next day before word of the assassination had gotten out 80 men from Shechem, Shiloh, and Samaria (cities of the Northern kingdom) who are traveling toward Jerusalem with offerings of grain, oil, and incense are intercepted by Ishmael. These men were in mourning and Ishmael appears to join them in their remorse. Ishmael convinces them to come to Mizpah where he slaughters all but 10 who bargain for their lives with the promise of grain and oil.

v.9 The cistern where the slain bodies are thrown had originally been dug by Asa for protection against the attacks by Baasha (**1 Kings 15:22 & 2 Chron. 16:6**). Any way you look at it the killing of these pilgrims was senseless.

v.10 Ishmael then takes the remainder of the inhabitants of Mizpah hostage as he flees to the Ammonites (See 40:13).

vv.11-15 When Johanan, who had warned Gedaliah of the assassin-nation plot, heard what Ishmael had done he gathered troops and pursued Ishmael. He caught up with him at the pool in Gibeon. [Interestingly, this is the location where David's troops under the command of Joab met up and fought with Ishbosheth's troops under the command of Abner in the days prior to David being king over all of Israel.] Somehow the hostages were able to escape from Ishmael and join themselves to Johanan and his troops. Ishmael and 8 of his men escape to the Ammonites.

vv.16-18 Johanan took the people he had rescued (this would have included Jeremiah as he had been staying in Mizpah under the protection of Gedaliah.) and went as far as Chimham (near Bethlehem) as they begin a journey to Egypt for fear of retaliation from Babylon.

Chapter 42

The Request

vv.1-3 The commanders and the people asked Jeremiah to petition God as to what they should do next. To demonstrate their desperation they said, "We are only a few left out of a multitude."

v.4 Jeremiah assures them that he will go to God for them and that he will hold nothing back of all the Lord tells him.

vv.5,6 The people then vow to do whatever the Lord says. It does not matter if it is good or bad they are determined to obey God.

The Response

v.7 After 10 days Jeremiah receives God's message for the people.

v.8 Jeremiah then calls all the people, lowly and great, to hear the message that has come from God in response to their request.

vv.9-12 God says, "Stay in the land. I will relent of the disasters I have sworn. You need not fear the king of Babylon. I will protect you from him. I will show you mercy if you will stay."

v.13 To not stay would be to disobey God.

vv.14-19 Jeremiah then gives the other side of the message. Do not go to Egypt thinking that you will escape war and famine there. What you dread here will surely follow you there. If you go to Egypt, you will die in Egypt. If you go to Egypt you will feel God's wrath as surely as the inhabitants of Jerusalem did.

v.20 Jeremiah then tells this people that their request was all a sham. They never intended to follow the will of God unless he told them to do what they had already decided to do.

vv.21,22 You have not obeyed the word of the Lord. You will die by the sword, pestilence, and famine in the land you desire (Egypt).

Chapter 43

vv.1,2 The message of God delivered by Jeremiah in chapter 42 is rejected by the proud, arrogant, former military leaders who have taken over following the death of Gedaliah. (They even accuse Jeremiah of lying to them.)

v.3 These leaders even ridiculously say that Jeremiah got this message from Baruch instead of from God. They even went so far as to say that upright Baruch was plotting with the Babylonians to get them killed.

vv.4-7 Johanan and the other captains would not obey the word of the Lord and stay in Judah. Instead they gathered up all the refugees who had fled to Judah as well as the remnant left behind by the Babylonians (this included those placed under the care and protection of Gedaliah) and fled to Egypt (Tahpanhes). [Jeremiah and Baruch most likely went as captives.]

vv.8,9 In Egypt God tells Jeremiah to place Large stones under the paving in the palace courtyard. He is to do this in plain view.

v.10 The message is God will bring Nebuchadnezzar against Egypt and he will set up his throne and pavilion over those very stones.

v.11 When Nebuchadnezzar comes he will strike Egypt and those destined for death, captivity, and sword will receive their reward.

vv.12,13 Egypt will be burned, captives will be taken. Egypt will be picked clean like a shepherd picking vermin and lice out of his cloak. This will happen as easily as a shepherd putting on his cloak.

NOTES

Chapter 44

v.1 Jeremiah is given one last message for these Jews who have fled to Egypt.

vv.2-6 Here he gives a quick review of recent history. Do you remember what you just saw happen in Judah? Think about how desolate that land is now. All of that happened because of wickedness and provoking God to anger. All of those people had been warned by God's prophets but refused to listen. Now Judah is a wasteland,

v.7 Why are you sinning against yourselves? (Sin does the most damage to the sinner.) Why have you now left no one in Judah?

v.8 You also provoke God's anger by your continued practice of idolatry here in Egypt.

vv.9-14 You are carrying on just like your fathers did. You have learned nothing. God will consume you as he did them. It will be so bad other nations will use Judah as a curse. No one will survive to go home again. A few may make it but very few.

v.15 This verse begins the response of the guilty; the men who knew that their wives were practicing idolatry and the women who were standing by.

v.16 "Even though you say that you are delivering God's message, we will not listen to you!"

v.17 "We will keep our vow to sacrifice to the queen of heaven like we used to do. We remember that we had plenty of bread then."

v.18 "Things have only gotten bad for us since we stopped worshipping her."

v.19 {Now the women speak up.} All of our worship to the queen of heaven was done with the knowledge and permission of our husbands.

vv.20-23 God knew what you were doing. When he got fed up with your rebellion he made your land a desolation. It was this behavior of yours that got you into this mess.

vv.24-28 God says you have made your choice. You prefer to keep your vows to the queen of heaven. Don't swear by my name any more. I will bring adversity and not good against you. The men of Judah will be consumed in Egypt, though a few may escape. Then you will know who is right; God or Astarte.

vv.29,30 You will know that this is true for I will turn Hophra over to his enemies like I turned Zedekiah over to Nebuchadnezzar.

Chapter 45

The Events of this Chapter Follow those of Chapter 36. You May Want to Review those Events to Get a Feel for What is Happening Here.

v.1 This is God's message for Baruch, the man who recorded Jeremiah's words in a book as well as helping Jeremiah with the land deal. This message came to Baruch after he had completed the writing of Jeremiah's words in the days of Jehoiakim.

vv.2,3 Baruch is greatly distressed as Jeremiah has been. He has been reminded of the prophesies which have been delivered by Jeremiah. He has been with Jeremiah and seen all Jeremiah had seen. It seems that there is nowhere to turn.

v.4 God reminds that he had built all this up and now he is going to tear it down.

v.5 There will be no greatness or honor for anyone in Israel but God assures Baruch that he will spare his life.

NOTES

Chapter 46

v.1 This chapter begins a series of judgments of God against nations that surround Judah. (Jeremiah, as other O.T. prophets brings judgments against other oppressing nations as well as his primary ministry to Judah.)

v.2 The 1st of these judgments deals with God's message to Egypt in the days of Pharaoh Necho. In the 4th year of Jehoiakim the Egyptian forces went out against the Babylonians at the battle of Charchemesh. While the Egyptians enjoyed early victory they were defeated by the forces under Nebuchadnezzar. [This is probably the time when the siege was lifted and the Babylonians were fighting the Egyptian army in chapter 37.]

vv.3,4 These verses picture the preparation to go into battle. The army is mighty in appearance with shiny armor.

vv.5,6 This is a picture totally opposite to the previous one. Here we see terror, retreat, panic, and defeat.

vv.7,8 This is in essence a song of pride going into the battle. We will cover the earth like a flood. Nothing can stand in our way.

v.9 This is a listing of some of the mighty mercenary forces under the command. of the Egyptians.

v.10 The battle really belongs to the Lord. This is a time in which he will avenge himself on his adversaries.

vv.11,12 There is no cure for Egypt's ills. The mighty will be soundly defeated and flee in shame. [This is a major contrast to the pride of vv.7,8.]

v.13 Not only will the Egyptians be defeated in Babylon, the Babylonians will come against Egypt and they will be defeated at home as well.

v.14 Get ready major cities.

v.15 The valiant were unable to stand for God brought them down.

v.16 They fall over one another scrambling to get away.

v.17 Pharaoh is all talk and no action.

v.18 Your enemies will tower over you.

v.19 Get ready to go into captivity.

vv.20,21 The mercenaries look powerful but in reality are only cattle fattened for slaughter. They are headed to the butcher.

vv.22,23 Egypt can only hiss and run like a snake in the woods when the forest is being cut down by the lumber company. Babylon will clear out in front of them like a swarm of locusts.

v.24 Egypt will be defeated in shame.

vv.25,26 Egypt's gods will fail so the Egyptians will be delivered into the hand of Nebuchadnezzar. But after her punishment Egypt will once again be restored.

vv.27,28 Jacob will be brought back from her captivity when God brings an end to the oppressing nations. Jacob will not be brought to a complete end but will be punished.

Chapter 47

v.1 This is one of the dated prophecies in the book. This message came to Jeremiah for the Philistines before Pharaoh Necho attacked and subdued Gaza (Philistia) on his march North to meet the Babylonians at Carchemish. This would be during the final years of Josiah. The destruction prophesied in this chapter will take place approximately 20 years later.

v.2 Destruction is coming from the North (Babylon). When it comes it will be as destructive as a flash flood. The Babylonians will roll over everything in their way. The devastation will be terrible.

v.3 The invading army with their war horses and chariots will be so terrifying parents will neglect their children as they seek to save themselves. The strong will be turned into weaklings by fear.

v.4 [The Philistines were a sea going people originally from the area of Crete (Caphtor).] All of Philistia will be plundered. Apparently, at one time there had been an alliance between Philistia and Tyre and Sidon. This alliance will be no more. Philistia will not even be able to help themselves.

v.5 Head shaving was a sign of humble mourning while the cutting of oneself was a part of pagan worship used as a sign of humility as one made supplication to their god (see contest on Mt. Carmel in **1 Kings 18**). The message of this verse is that all of this is useless for their defeat is sure.

vv.6,7 The sword of the Lord (God's vengeance) will not cease until the Philistines are totally defeated.

NOTES

Chapter 48

God's Judgment Against Moab

v.1 Nebo is the mountain from which Moses was allowed to view the promised land. This was a prominent point in the land of Moab. In this prophecy Nebo is laid waste, Kirjathaim is shamed and taken. All of the fortresses and strongholds will be shamed, dismayed, and destroyed.

v.2 No one will honor Moab. In Heshbon plans are made for the overthrow of this nation. After this defeat all will be quiet for all that will be left is silence as in Madmen (a city of Moab whose name means quiet).

v.3 The cry will go up that Horonaim is destroyed with great destruction.

vv.4,5 The cry goes up that Moab is destroyed. Even the little children are taken in a forced march up Luhith and down to Horonaim in hopes of escape. Still they hear the distressed cry of destruction.

v.6 "Run save yourself. Become like a juniper in the desert." [The juniper is a plant that can withstand drought and grows well in an arid climate.]

v.7 Because they trusted in their own strength and did not depend upon God and worshipped the idol, Chemosh, they will be taken away along with their false god and his priests.

vv.8,9 Every city will perish for all the country will be destroyed and a desolation.

v.10 God expects the conquering army to come with full force and not let up until the job is done.

vv.11,12 Moab had been allowed a peaceful existence. They had been as undisturbed as wine left to age. The day is coming when the wine of their existence will be disturbed and their jar broken.

v.13 They will be ashamed of Chemosh who could not save them anymore than the golden calf at Bethel had been able to save Israel.

vv.14-16 Moab may have been known as having strong men of war but when the destroyer sent by God comes the mightiest of men will go down to slaughter and that time of calamity is near.

v.17 The nations around Moab will mourn and grieve that the mighty scepter of Moab is broken.

vv.18,19 The inhabitants of the land will only be able to sit in the dust and ask what happened as they see their cities destroyed.

v.20 Moab is laid waste. (The Arnon is a major river on the border of Moab.)

vv.21-25 Judgment is brought against all the cities of the land (this indicates the complete destruction God is bringing). Her strength is gone (her horn is cut off and arm broken).

vv.26,27 God will render Moab helpless (drunk and vomiting). He will turn it into a derision {a cause for laughter}. They had laughed at Israel and treated them like criminals caught in the act.

v.28 Run to the caves to hide!

vv.29,30 Moab had been boastful but it was a false pride and they could not back it up.

vv.31-33 At one time Moab had been a place of beautiful vineyards. Now, all is destroyed.

v.34 The whole land has become desolate and without direction.

v.35 Moab was destroyed for their idolatry.

v.36 Moan and weep for Moab.

vv.37-39 Now all the people of Moab lament, weep, and are in deep sorrow as is evidenced by the shaved heads and beards and the sack cloth. Moab is broken like a vessel no one wants.

vv.40,41 The attackers will come on Moab as swift as eagles and the cities will be taken. The very heart of Moab's warriors will melt and they will be turned to weaklings.

v.42 Moab will be destroyed because they magnified themselves against the Lord.

vv.43,44 Terror, pit, and snare await Moab. If they escape one they will be caught by another.

v.45 The fugitives pause in the light of the fires of Heshbon.

v.46 Woe to Moab for all her children are taken captive.

v.47 In later times Moab will be restored.

NOTES

Chapter 49

Rather than Just Containing God's Judgment Against One Nation, this Chapter Contains Five Separate Judgments. By the Time We Finish these Last Chapters of Jeremiah We will have Seen God's Judgments Against all of Mesopotamia from Egypt to Elam.

AMMON

v.1 Does Israel have no one to inherit their land? Why have the Ammonites presumptuously taken over what previously had been Israelite territory? [Milcom or Molech was an Ammonite deity. Gad was one of the tribes that settled east of the Jordan.]

v.2 The day is coming when God will bring war against Ammon. The cities will be destroyed and Israel will take her territory back.

v.3 Wail, cry, put on sack cloth (sign of distress). Their god will be taken along with the priests.

v.4 Why do you boast of your great riches? (They will not save them.)

v.5 Terror is coming on you from all sides and no one will be around to gather the wanderers (fugitives).

v.6 Afterward Ammon's fortunes will be restored.

EDOM

v.7 All wisdom seems to have departed from Edom.

v.8 Run and hide for disaster is planned for Esau.

vv.9,10 Where harvesters might leave some grapes behind and thieves might not clean you out, I will strip you bare. All of your hiding places will be gone and all of the people will be no more.

v.11 I will care for the widows and orphans.

v.12 If those who do not deserve to drink the cup of punishment drink it, why should you go unpunished? You deserve it. {If Israel did not go unpunished and they were better than you then why do you think that you will escape?}

v.13 All the cities will be left in ruins.

v.14 All of the surrounding nations have been called to destroy Edom.

v.15 You will be made small among the nations (a nobody).

v.16 Your pride and the stronghold you live in has deceived you. You may live in a mountain fortress but I will bring you down.

v.17 All who pass by will be horrified.

v.18 No one will dwell in your cities. They will be as desolate as Sodom and Gomorrah.

vv.19,20 God will come against Edom like a lion cleaning out a flock of sheep.

v.21 The news of Edom's destruction will be widely known.

v.22 The enemy will swoop down like an eagle and instill tremendous fear and pain on Edom's warriors.

DAMASCUS

vv.23,24 All Syria is dismayed by the news of impending destructtion. All hope is gone.

v.25 Why haven't you run while you could?

v.26 All the young men will be slaughtered.

v.27 All of Damascus will be burned up.

KEDAR & HAZOR

v.28 This is God's call for Nebuchadnezzar to attack these desert villages.

v.29 All they have will be taken. There will be terror on every side.

v.30 Run to the caves to hide.

v.31 While they had been at ease they had been easy pickings.

v.32 All they have is now plunder.

v.33 They will be so totally wiped out that no one but jackals and other scavengers will ever live there again.

ELAM

v.34 This message came to Jeremiah in the last days of Judah during the reign of Zedekiah.

v.35 Elam's might and strength will be broken.

v.36 Elamites will be scattered to nations all around them. They will be scattered to the 4 winds.

v.37 Elam will be scattered in God's anger and wrath until they are brought to an end.

v.38 King and official will be destroyed.

v.39 Still, Elam's fortunes will one day be restored.

NOTES

Chapter 50

Chapters 50 and 51 Deal with God's Judgment Against Babylon

v.1 At this point Jeremiah gives God's judgment against Babylon.

v.2 Declare Babylon is fallen. [Bel and Marduk (Merodach) were the idol gods of the Babylonians.] God declares shame and destruction against these gods that cannot save.

v.3 A nation from the North (Media) will attack and make the land desolate. All will be wiped out.

vv.4,5 Here we have a picture of the repentance and return of the captives of Israel. Those who had rejected God and broken their covenant with God now seek him and a perpetual covenant.

vv.6,7 In these verses we see an explanation of why Israel was taken into captivity. Israel had had bad shepherds (prophets, priests, and kings) who had failed to lead in the right way and protect the sheep from the enemies. As a result they had been devoured by the enemy. They were in captivity and defeated because they had sinned against the God of their refuge.

v.8 Israel is warned to flee Babylon for God is bringing an assembly of nations to plunder Babylon.

vv.9,10 The nation that attacks will be like sharpshooters in that they always get what they aim for. The plunderers will get all that they want.

v.11 Babylon's pride has led to her downfall. {Remember Nebuchadnezzar's period of insanity and Belshazzar's party (**Daniel chapters 4 and 5**).}

v.12 Mighty Babylon will be turned into a puny wasteland.

v.13 Because of God's wrath Babylon will no longer be inhabited. It will be desolate [This is much the same thing they had done to Jerusalem only Babylon's fate is permanent.]

vv.14-16 Spare no ammunition. Tear her down. Do to her as she has done to others. There will be no more planting or harvest.

v.17 Israel had been like sheep (prey for the lions of Assyria and Babylon).

vv.18-20 Israel will be restored. Babylon will be punished. Peace will return to the mountains and valleys of Israel and her iniquity will be forgiven.

vv.21,22 This is God's call for the attack on Babylon.

v.23 God's hammer is now broken. [God had used Babylon as a hammer to punish other nations. Now Babylon is destroyed.]

v.24 Babylon had fallen into this trap because they fought against God.

vv.25-27 God is turning his fury loose to the point that Babylon will be totally destroyed, man and beast.

v.28 The refugees will sing the song of God's vengeance in Zion.

v.29 Give to her as she has given to others. {Babylon is simply harvesting what they had sown.}

v.30 All the men of Babylon will fall.

vv.31,32 God is against proud, haughty Babylon. She will fall never to rise again.

vv.33,34 This is God's promised delivery of Israel.

vv.35-37 The sword of God will be brought against the rulers, soothsayers, mighty men, horses, chariots, mixed multitudes, and treasure. In short all of Babylon will feel God's wrath.

v.38 Drought will come against this idolatrous nation. (The army of Cyrus marched into Babylon by means of the dried riverbed of the Euphrates after having re-routed the river.)

vv.39,40 No man will ever live in Babylon again. (It will be home only to jackals and other scavenging animals. [The unclean.]) {Sodom and Gomorrah are uninhabitable as they are under the Dead Sea.}

vv.41,42 A fierce nation will come against Babylon.

v.43 Babylon's king will lose all strength. {See Belshazzar in **Daniel 5**.}

v.44 God's vengeance will be like a lion scattering and destroying the flock with no shepherd to stop him.

vv.45,46 Even the weakest will be taken and the earth will tremble at the news of the fall of mighty Babylon.

NOTES

Chapter 51

This Chapter is a Continuation of God's Judgment Against Babylon. Babylon has been the Feared Nation that Defeated Others. Now Her Time is Come.

vv.1,2 God's cleansing wind is coming to blow away the chaff that is Babylon. The day of doom is coming when other nations will winnow her.

v.3 The attack will be sudden. The Babylonians won't have time to prepare themselves for battle.

v.4 The slain will fall in the streets.

v.5 This is evidence that God has neither forgotten nor forsaken his people.

v.6 Run away for this will be the time of God's vengeance and it will be complete.

vv.7-9 Babylon had been God's tool to punish other nations. Now their time has come and there is no balm, no healing for her.

v.10 "The Lord has vindicated us! Shout it aloud in Zion (Jerusalem)."

vv.11,12 The message is addressed to Babylon once again as God tells her to prepare for the battle for God has aroused the king of the Medes. [See **Dan. 5:30**] Set up your guard for God is doing what he promised.

v.13 Babylon, your time has come.

v.14 God will fill Babylon with invading armies as destructive as locusts.

vv.15,16 God, the creator, is a God of power and might. He is in control of all of nature.

vv.17,18 Idol worshippers are dull-brained. The molded image is a lie. They are useless.

v.19 God, on the other hand, is the maker of all things and not made by some metal-smith. [See **Acts 17:24,25**]

vv.20-23 Babylon had been God's tool of destruction (hammer).

v.24 Now Babylon will be repaid for all the evil they have done. They will pay for the destruction of Jerusalem.

v.25 God is against this destroying nation.

v.26 When God is finished with them they will be a burned out shell and no one will even use a single brick for other construction.

vv.27-29 Call the nations to battle under the leadership of the Medes; A powerful army to carry out God's purpose.

v.30 Babylon's mighty men lose their will to fight as all the strongholds of the city are destroyed.

vv.31,32 Messengers from all areas of the city bring the news of total defeat. All that was great is no more.

v.33 Babylon is ripe for her defeat; set to fall.

vv.34,35 This is the cry for vengeance from the captives of Judah.

vv.36-40 God has heard their cry and will bring his vengeance against Babylon to the point that what was once a great city will now be uninhabitable. Though they roar like lions they will be tamed and slaughtered like sheep.

vv.41-43 Babylon will be wiped out as by a flood. [Think of the devastation caused by the storm surge during a hurricane.]

v.44 Bel is one of the pagan god's of Babylon. The message is Babylon will be forced to give up all they have taken or devoured.

vv.45,46 Believe the rumors and flee to escape God's fierce anger.

vv.47,48 God will bring his vengeance and show his supremacy over all of Babylon's idols and as the result all heaven and earth will rejoice.

v.49 Babylon will be made to pay for all of her wickedness as well as her atrocities toward all the nations.

v.50 If you are able to get away, flee. Remember what happened in Jerusalem.

vv.51,52 Babylon will pay for defiling the temple when God brings his judgment against all of her idols.

v.53 Any fortifications Babylon can come up with will be useless.

vv.54-57 The cry will arise in Babylon as God's vengeance is poured out and the plunderers are turned loose. All the mighty will fall. God is repaying them for their wickedness. God will bring an end to all their leaders.

v.58 Babylon will be completely destroyed and the nations will not be able to put out the fire of God's wrath.

vv.59-64 As Seraiah, King Zedekiah's quartermaster, {and Baruch's brother?} is taken to Babylon, Jeremiah gives him a book of the prophecy of Babylon's fall. When he arrives in Babylon he is to read the book aloud then sink it in the Euphrates river signifying that mighty Babylon will sink to rise no more.

NOTES

Chapter 52

This Chapter Recounts the Fall of Jerusalem as Well as the Final Days of Zedekiah and Jehoiachin. These Events are also Covered in 2 Kings 24 & 25

v.1 Zedekiah became king at the age of 21 and reigned 11 years.

v.2 Zedekiah chose to follow in the idolatrous practices of his predecessors.

v.3 Because of God's anger at the rebellion of Judah he allowed Jerusalem to fall. The final siege was brought on by Zedekiah's rebellion against Babylon. [Apparently, for a time Zedekiah had served as a vassal to Babylon. (See 51:59)]

v.4 In the 9th year of Zedekiah's reign Nebuchadnezzar brought the whole Babylonian army and laid siege to Jerusalem.

vv.5,6 The siege lasted approximately one and one half years. By the end the blockade had been so successful all food was gone from the city.

v.7 Then the city wall was breached. Zedekiah and his army tried to escape by sneaking away through a passage between the walls. This in spite of the fact that the city was completely surrounded by Babylonian troops at the time.

v.8 Zedekiah was captured at Jericho and his army scattered away.

vv.9-11 Zedekiah is then taken to be tried before Nebuchadnezzar at Riblah. After his judgment is pronounced he is forced to watch as his sons are slaughtered then has his eyes put out. He is then taken in chains to Babylon where he is imprisoned until his death.

vv.12-14 Nebuzaradan then came into the city and burned all of the prominent houses including the temple and the homes of the king and officials of Judah . The army was then ordered to tear the walls down. Jerusalem is truly being turned into a pile of rubble.

vv.15,16 The last group of captives are rounded up and sent to Babylon. Only a few of the poorest are left to tend vineyards.

vv.17-23 Everything of value left on and in the temple is taken at this time. The bronze pillars and the bronze sea are broken up to be hauled back to Babylon. These pillars were 27 ft. high and 18 ft. in circumference and 3 in. thick (hollow).

vv.24-27 Seraiah the High Priest, Zephaniah the 2nd priest, and the rest of the officials left in Jerusalem were gathered and taken to Riblah where they were executed.

vv.28-30 These verses give a breakdown of the number of captives taken each of the three times Nebuchadnezzar took captives of Judah. [The reason this number seems smaller is because this was a count of men of military age.]

vv.31-34 After Jehoiachin had been a captive 37 years (was 18 when taken), Evil-Merodach, successor to Nebuchadnezzar, brought him out of prison. He was elevated to a place of prominence among all the other captive kings and was even given an allowance for the rest of his life.

www.ingramcontent.com/pod-product-compliance
Lightning Source LLC
Chambersburg PA
CBHW060834050426
42453CB00008B/691